United States
Department of
Agriculture

Forest Service

Southern
Research Station

Resource Bulletin
SRS–186

Southern Pulpwood Production, 2010 (revised)

James W. Bentley and
Carolyn D. Steppleton

Note: All tables in this report are available in Microsoft® Excel workbook files. Upon request these files will be supplied in the format the customer requests.

The use of trade or firm names in this publication is for reader information and does not imply endorsement by the U.S. Department of Agriculture of any product or service.

Front cover: Load of pulp logs headed to pulpmill in central Alabama. (photo by James W. Bentley)

Revised due to: The unit received some incorrect productions numbers for the 2010 data. The unit has reprocessed the 2010 data with the correct numbers and revised the report.

www.srs.fs.usda.gov

March 2012
Revised—August 2012

Southern Research Station
200 W.T. Weaver Blvd.
Asheville, NC 28804

Southern Pulpwood Production, 2010

James W. Bentley, Forester
Forest Inventory and Analysis
Forest Service, Southern Research Station
U.S. Department of Agriculture, Knoxville, TN

and

Carolyn D. Steppleton, Statistical Assistant
Forest Inventory and Analysis
Forest Service, Southern Research Station
U.S. Department of Agriculture, Asheville, NC

Introduction

The Forest Inventory and Analysis (FIA) unit of the Southern Research Station annually compiles, analyzes, and reports canvass data of pulpmills in the South. This report for 2010 presents the findings of a 100-percent canvass of pulpmills that drew roundwood or wood residues from the 13 Southern States. Of the 82 mills canvassed, 81 responded. For the one mill that did not respond, previous canvass data and other sources of information were used for the findings reported in this publication. Regional conversion factors were used to convert mill data reported in nonstandard units to standard cords. The report gives all production figures in cords and does not include pulpwood that is exported out of the country. Tables A.1, A.2, and A.6 through A.18 of the report express equivalent green tons of production. Unless otherwise indicated, the context for production comparisons (increases, decreases, or stabilizations) throughout the report is the change from 2009 to 2010.

Pulpwood

Total Southern pulpwood production, which includes both roundwood chipped at pulpmills or at independent chipmills and other primary industry mill residues, was up 7 percent, 4.4 million cords, to 65.5 million cords (174.3 million green tons) (table A.1). This increase comes after a decline in 2009 and puts total production slightly below the level seen in 2008. At 48.2 million cords, softwood production increased 2.8 million cords, or 6 percent. Hardwood production was up 10 percent, from 15.7 to 17.3 million cords. Softwood roundwood and residues combined accounted for 74 percent of the total Southern pulpwood production, while hardwoods accounted for the remaining 26 percent (table A.2). Total Southern pulpwood production was 14 percent lower than the record volume of 75.9 million cords (200.9 million green tons) reported in 1997.

Pulpwood production in the South Central region (Alabama, Arkansas, Kentucky, Louisiana, Mississippi, Oklahoma, Tennessee, and Texas) increased 9 percent, from 31.7 to 34.7 million cords. Softwood pulpwood production was up 2.0 million cords, or nearly 9 percent, in the region, while hardwood production increased 997,000 cords, or 11 percent. The South Central region's production was down 18 percent, or 7.9 million cords (20.2 million green tons) from the peak year of 1997. Between 1997 and 2010, the South Central region lost 15 pulpmills and 13 percent of its pulping capacity. This region accounts for 53 percent of the South's total pulping capacity.

Production in the Southeast (Florida, Georgia, North Carolina, South Carolina, and Virginia) increased 5 percent, from 29.5 million cords to 30.9 million cords. Softwood production was up 3 percent in this region, or 803,852 cords, while hardwood production increased 10 percent, or 612,696 cords. From its peak year of 1997, the Southeast region's production declined 7 percent, or 2.5 million cords (6.4 million green tons). Between 1997 and 2010, the Southeast lost six pulpmills and 12 percent of its pulping capacity.

Georgia's pulpwood production was up 14 percent to 11.4 million cords, leading the South in total pulpwood production (fig. 1). Alabama's production was up 8 percent to 10.2 million cords. Production in Mississippi increased 16

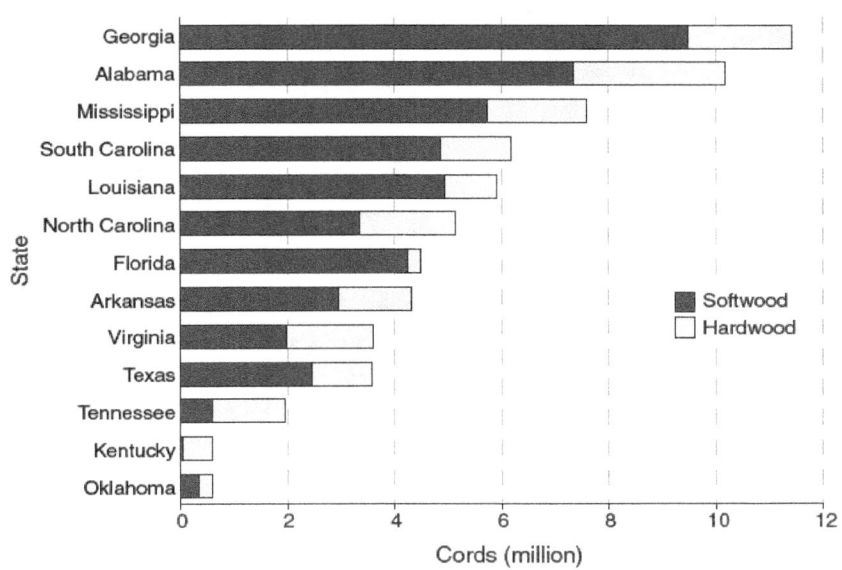

Figure 1—Pulpwood production by State and broad species, 2010.

percent to 7.6 million cords. Pulpwood production in South Carolina dropped 4 percent to 6.2 million cords. Louisiana's and North Carolina's production was up 3 and 6 percent to 5.9 and 5.1 million cords, respectively. Collectively, these six States accounted for 46.4 million cords, or 71 percent, of the South's total 2010 production.

Roundwood

Roundwood pulpwood continues to be the primary fiber source used in pulp manufacture in the South. In 2010, it accounted for 78 percent of the total Southern pulpwood production (fig. 2). This represents an increase over 2009 when roundwood accounted for 76 percent of total pulpwood production. Between 2003 and 2006, roundwood comprised between 72 and 74 percent. Overall, from 2009 to 2010, the South's roundwood production increased by 4.5 million cords, or 10 percent, from 46.5 to 51.0 million cords (table A.3). At 37.1 million cords, softwood accounted for nearly 73 percent of the total roundwood production. Between 2009 and 2010, softwood roundwood production was up by 8 percent, or 2.9 million cords, while hardwood roundwood production increased by 1.6 million cords, or 13 percent. In comparison to the peak year of 1997, softwood roundwood production was up by 3.1 million cords, or 9 percent, while hardwood roundwood production dropped by 6.3 million cords, or 31 percent.

Eleven Southern States—Alabama, Arkansas, Georgia, Kentucky, Louisiana, Mississippi, North Carolina, Oklahoma, Tennessee, Texas, and Virginia—showed a increase in roundwood production, with respective increases ranging from 2 to 27 percent. Two Southern States showed small to moderate declines in roundwood production. Georgia's roundwood production was up 16 percent and still led in total roundwood production, with 9.3 million cords, and was the leading producer of softwood roundwood, with 7.7 million cords. At 8.0 million cords, Alabama ranked second in total roundwood production and was the leading producer of hardwood roundwood, at 2.4 million cords. Roundwood pulpwood production in Mississippi, Louisiana, South Carolina, and Florida was 6.3, 4.7, 4.7, and 3.5 million cords, respectively. Combined production in these six States was 36.5 million cords, for 71 percent of the South's roundwood total.

Wood Residues

Mills reported two types of receipts: roundwood and wood residues. Wood residues consist primarily of mill residue chips, a byproduct of sawmilling and veneer mill operations. This publication reports certain residues that technically are not wood residues, such as chips produced in the woods or generated when material received as roundwood by primary producers is chipped instead of milled.

Wood residue production in the South dropped <1 percent to 14.6 million cords, or 35.2 million tons (table A.4). Softwood residue production declined <1 percent to 11.2 million cords but still accounted for 77 percent of total wood residues. Hardwood residue production remained fairly stable at 3.4 million cords.

Seven Southern States—Arkansas, Florida, Georgia, Mississippi, North Carolina, Tennessee, and Texas—showed an increase in wood residue production, while six States showed moderate to substantial declines ranging from <1 to 72 percent. Alabama led Southern States in the production of wood residues with 2.2 million cords, followed by Georgia, North Carolina, South Carolina, Mississippi, and Louisiana with 2.1, 1.7, 1.5, 1.3, and 1.2 million cords, respectively. Combined wood residue production in these six States amounted to 9.9 million cords, or 68 percent of the South's total.

County and Parish Production

Table A.5 summarizes pulpwood production in the South by source of wood, State, year, and number of mills for 2000 through 2010. Tables A.6 through A.18 report county and parish (herein county) patterns of roundwood pulpwood production for domestic pulpmills. Exports of wood residues and pulpwood production exported outside the United States are not included in these figures because of difficulty determining the county of origin for the residues and exports. In 2010, of the 1,306 total counties in the 13 Southern States, 913 counties produced softwood or hardwood roundwood or

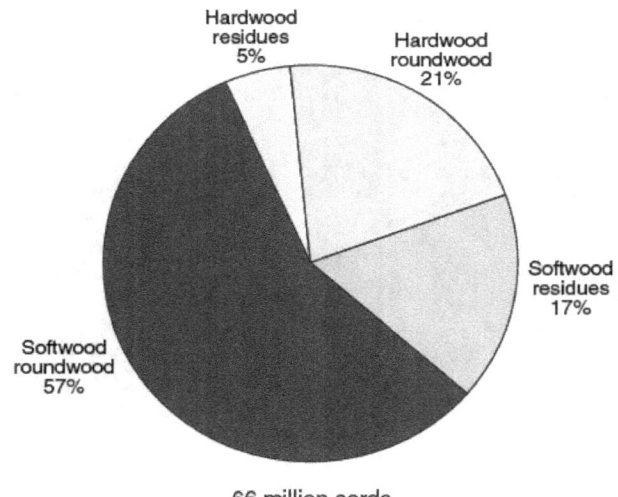

66 million cords

Figure 2—Softwood and hardwood components of Southern pulpwood production, 2010.

both; in 2009, this number was 902; in 2008, it was 891; and in 2007, it was 877.

Of counties producing in 2010, only 18, or 2 percent, harvested >250,000 cords of softwood and hardwood roundwood combined; 10 of the 19 counties were in Alabama and Louisiana. Sixteen percent, or 146 counties evenly distributed across the South, reported roundwood production ranging between 100,000 and 250,000 cords, while 191 counties, or 21 percent, reported production that ranged between 50,000 and 99,999 cords. The remaining 558 counties or 61 percent of producing counties produced <50,000 cords. Figures 3 and 4 depict the intensity of production of softwood and hardwood roundwood pulpwood in cords per acre of treated timberland, a measurement that discounts the effect

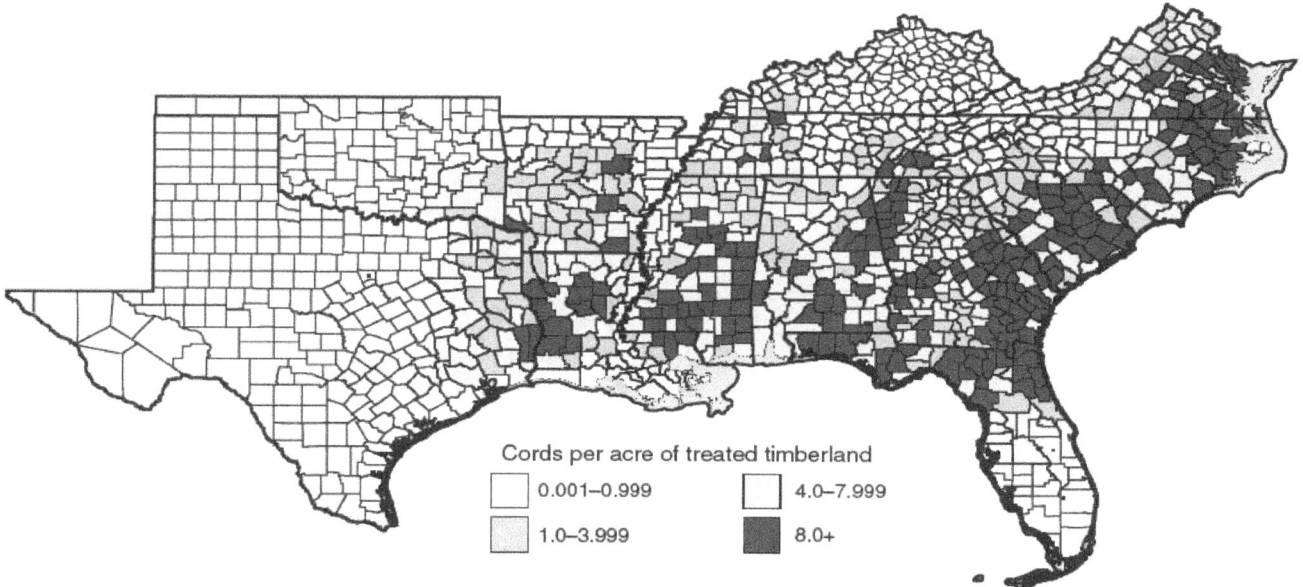

Figure 3—Softwood roundwood production in the South by county or parish, 2010.

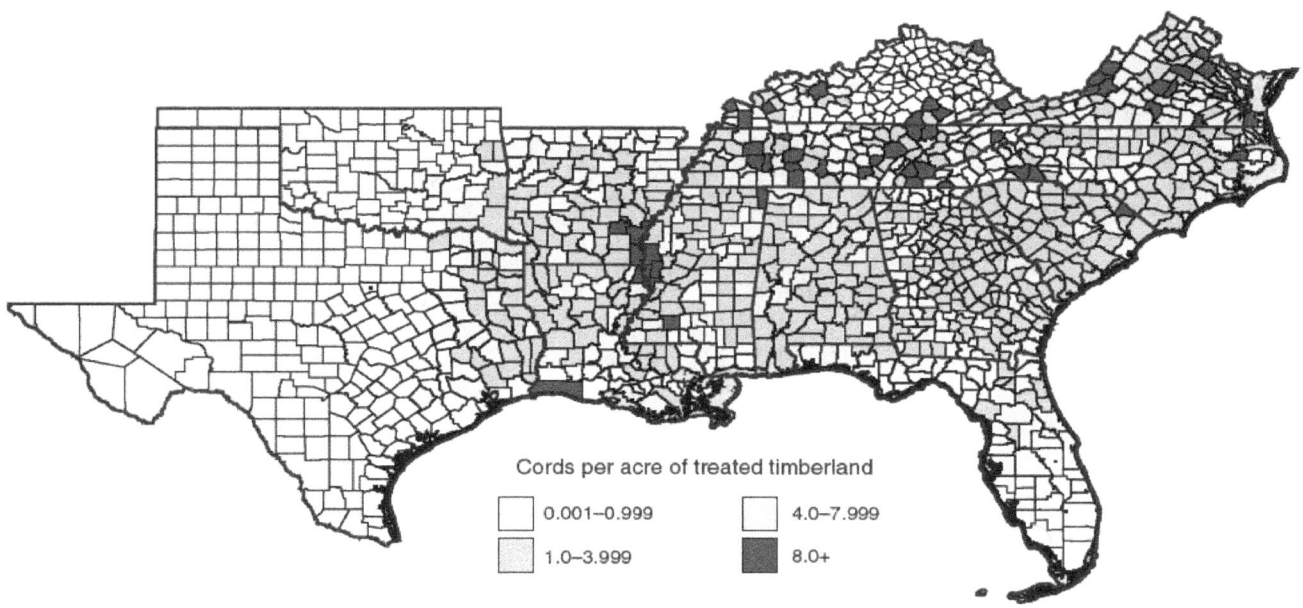

Figure 4—Hardwood roundwood production in the South by county or parish, 2010.

of county size on concentration of production. The reasoning behind and methodology for using treated acres versus total timberland area are discussed in McCollum.[1] In both figures, counties in the dark shade of blue produced >8 cords per acre of treated timberland. Across the South, 224 counties produced >8 cords of softwood per acre of treated timberland, while only 58 counties produced >8 cords of hardwood per acre of treated timberland (table 1).

Table 1—Number of producing counties in the South by range of cords per acre of treated timberland for softwood and hardwood roundwood, 2010

Range	Softwood	Hardwood
cords/treated acre	number of counties	
0	71	15
0.001–0.999	226	264
1.0–3.999	199	453
4.0–7.999	193	123
8.0+	224	58
Total	913	913

A barometer of local competition for pulpwood is the number of pulpmills procuring wood from each county (figs. 5 and 6). In 407, or 45 percent, of the producing counties, 1 to 3 mills were actively procuring both softwood and hardwood roundwood (table 2). In 343, or 37 percent, of the producing counties, 4 to 6 mills were actively procuring wood. In the remaining 163, or 18 percent, of producing counties, 7 or more mills were active. By comparison, in 1997, a peak year for Southern pulpwood production, 103 pulpmills were active in the South, and 347, or 38 percent, of producing counties had 7 or more mills competing for wood.

Roundwood Movement

Tables A.19 and A.20 show the domestic import and export volumes and roundwood movement of softwood and hardwood roundwood between States in the Southeast and South Central regions. Numbers in boxes represent roundwood harvested and retained for processing in each State. The numbers in rows to the left and right of the boxed numbers represent wood exported to the other States. Therefore, the sum of the figure for retained wood and the figure for exported wood is the total roundwood production for the

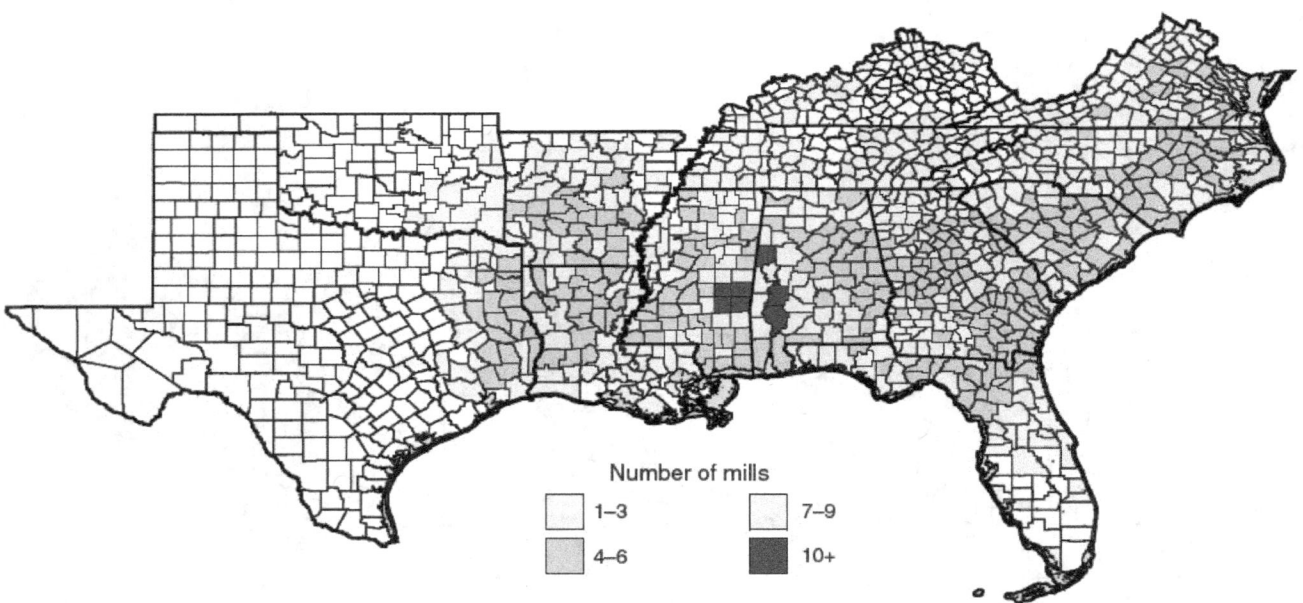

Number of mills

☐ 1–3   ☐ 7–9

☐ 4–6   ■ 10+

Figure 5—Number of mills competing for softwood roundwood by county or parish, 2010.

---

[1] McCollum, J M. Resolving the timber products output canvass with phase 2 data. Manuscript in preparation. McCollum can be reached at Southern Research Station, 4700 Old Kingston Pike, Knoxville, TN 37919.

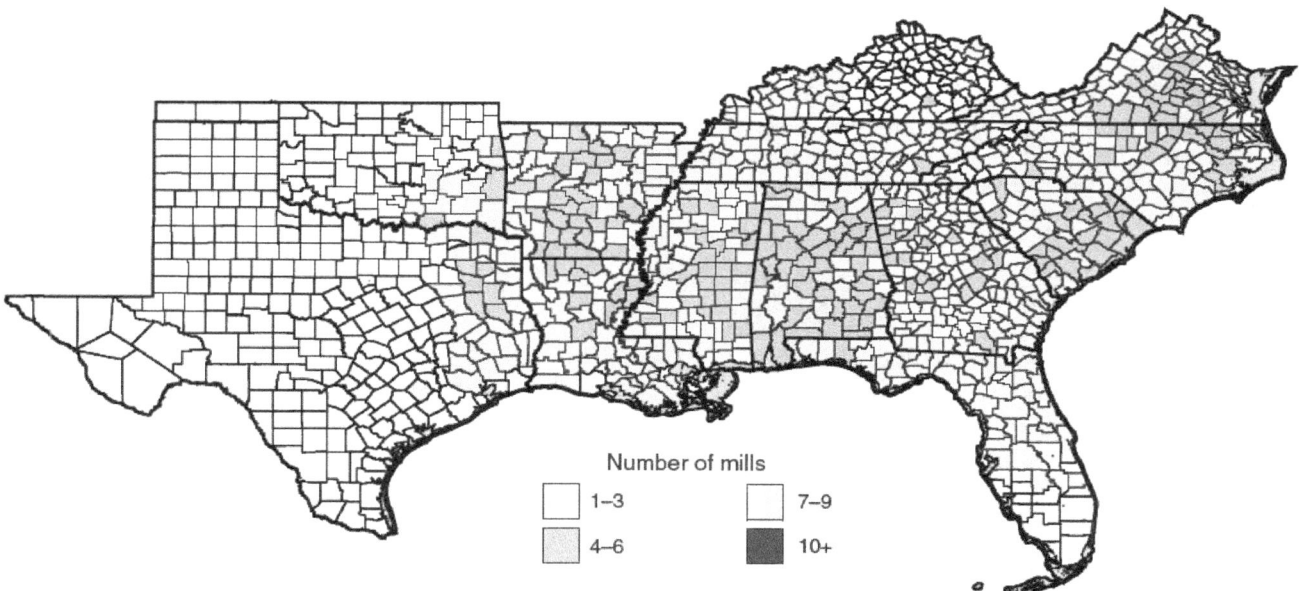

Figure 6—Number of mills competing for hardwood roundwood by county or parish, 2010.

Number of mills

☐ 1–3   ☐ 7–9

▨ 4–6   ■ 10+

Table 2—Number of producing counties in the South by number of pulpmills procuring softwood and hardwood roundwood, 2010

Mills	Combined[a]	Softwood[b]	Hardwood[c]
number	*number of counties*		
0	0	71	15
1–3	407	487	672
4–6	343	287	210
7–9	136	61	16
10+	27	7	0
Total	913	913	913

[a] Combined is counties with mills procuring both softwood and hardwood.

[b] Softwood is counties with mills procuring only softwood.

[c] Hardwood is counties with mills procuring only hardwood.

State. The numbers in columns either above or below the figures for retained wood represent wood imported from other States. The sum of the retained figure and the figure for wood imported from other States represents roundwood receipts or the amount of roundwood processed by mills in a State.

The South Central region was a net importer of roundwood pulpwood. For softwood and hardwood combined, imports exceeded exports by 60,601 cords (tables A.19 and A.20). Softwood exports exceeded imports by 413,139 cords, while hardwood imports exceeded exports by 473,740 cords. The Southeast was a net importer of pulpwood, with softwood and hardwood imports exceeding exports by 96,007 cords. Softwood imports exceeded exports by 243,960 cords, while hardwood exports exceeded imports by 147,953 cords. Across the South roundwood pulpwood receipts, or consumption, exceeded production by 156,608 cords.

Mills and Pulping Capacity

In 2010, 82 southern pulpmills were operating and drawing wood from the 13 Southern States, 1 less than in 2009 (fig. 7). The International Paper mill in Pineville, Louisiana closed in 2009. At the same time, total southern mill pulping capacity decreased from 123,368 tons per day in 2009 to 123,076 tons per day in 2010. Daily capacity of individual mills ranged from 125 to 4,750 tons. In 1979, 117 mills were operating in the South, where the average pulpmill capacity was 948 tons per day. By 1997, a peak year for pulpwood production in the South, the number of operating pulpmills in the South had declined to 103, but average pulping capacity had increased to 1,361 tons per day. In 2010, the average daily capacity was 1,501 tons per day, 15 tons per day higher than in 2009 and 140 tons per day higher than in 1997.

Many companies operate pulping facilities throughout the South. In 2009, International Paper Company was the dominant pulp and paper company, with 16 pulpmills in 10 Southern States responsible for 27 percent of the South's pulping capacity. Georgia-Pacific Corporation operated 10 pulpmills in seven States and accounted for 14 percent of the South's pulping capacity. Smurfit-Stone Container Corporation operated seven pulpmills in five States and accounted for 8 percent of the South's pulping capacity. With 60,811 tons of pulping capacity, these three companies were responsible for 49 percent of the South's pulping capacity. Domtar Paper Co., LLC, Temple-Inland, Inc., AbitibiBowater, Inc., Weyerhaeuser Company, and MeadWestvaco Corporation operated six, five, four, four, and three mills, respectively, and accounted for another 26 percent of the South's pulping capacity.

The sulfate process dominated the industry in 2010, accounting for 89 percent of mill capacity. Groundwood or other mechanical processes accounted for 5 percent, semi-chemical 5 percent, and soda and other chemical processes 1 percent (table A.21). These capacities have remained relatively stable over the past few years. Based on 2010 production and mill capacity, and using an average of 350 total operating days, southern pulpmills operated at 96-percent capacity.

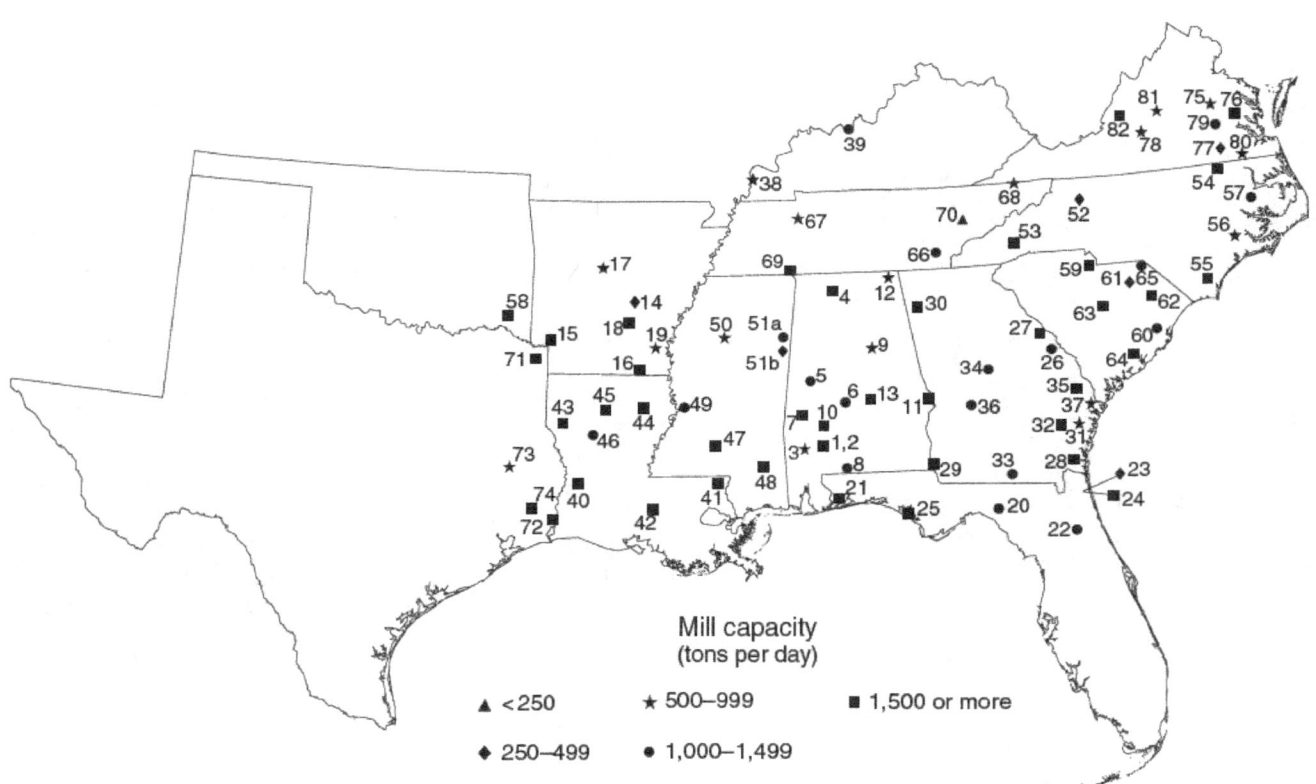

Figure 7—Capacity of southern pulpmills operating and drawing wood from the 13 Southern States, 2010. Numerals are coded on Table A.21.

Alabama and Georgia continued to lead the South in the number of operating mills, with 12 mills each. Alabama led in pulping capacity, with 22,722 tons per day and Georgia followed with 20,779 tons per day (table 3). These two States accounted for 35 percent of the South's pulping capacity. In addition, three pulpmills outside the Southern region drew wood from the South in 2010 (table A.22).

Trends

Figure 8 depicts Southern pulpwood production from 1953 to 2010. The 7-percent increase registered between 2009 and 2010 is one of the largest increases recorded since data collection began; second only to the 11-percent increase recorded between 1996 and 1997. Softwood roundwood expressed as a percent of total production declined significantly from 1953 until the mid-1980s. In 1953, softwood roundwood supplied 87 percent of the total pulpwood production. By 1985 it made-up only 44 percent of total production and remained relatively stable until 2002. Since then softwood roundwood

Table 3—Number of pulpmills and pulping capacity by State, 2010

State	Mills	24-hour capacity
	number	tons
Alabama	12	22,722
Arkansas	6	7,720
Florida	6	8,663
Georgia	12	20,779
Kentucky	2	2,250
Louisiana	7	13,320
Mississippi	6	8,054
North Carolina	6	8,270
Oklahoma	1	2,075
South Carolina	7	10,183
Tennessee	5	4,955
Texas	4	5,937
Virginia	8	8,148
Total	82	123,076

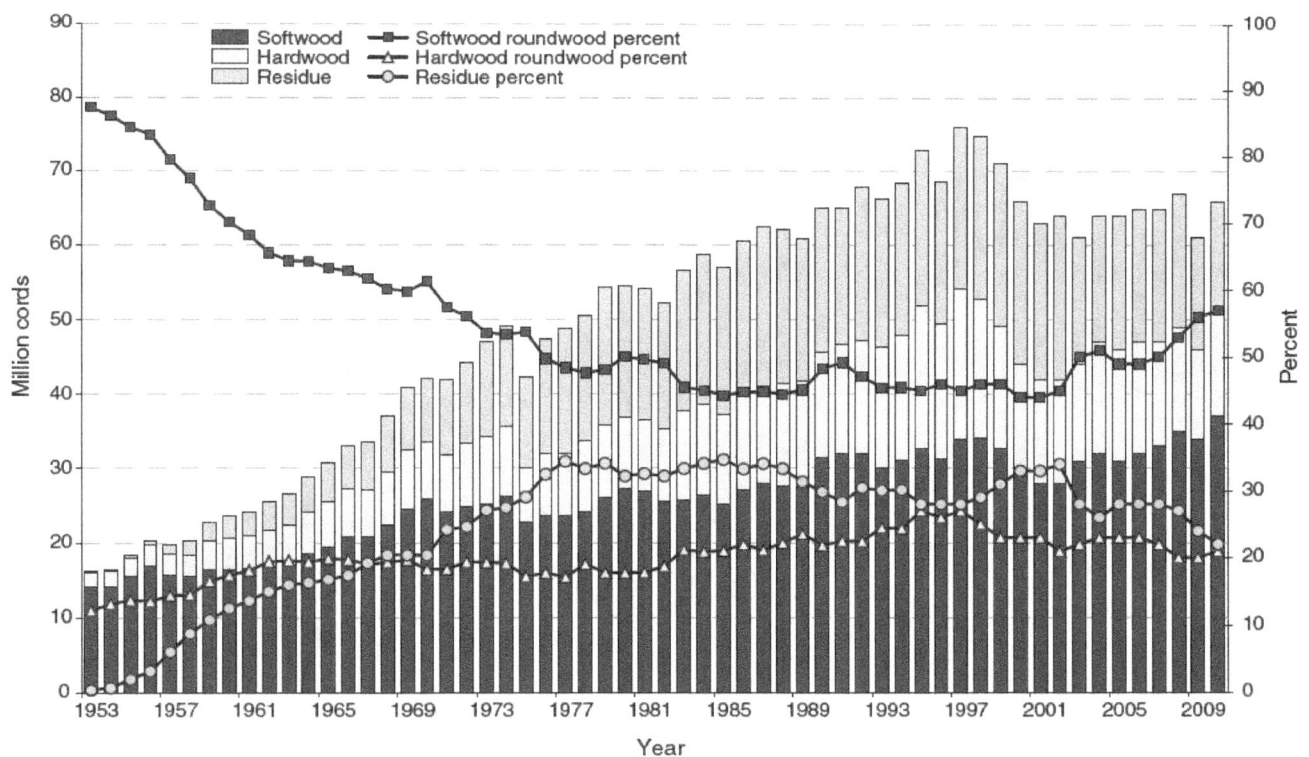

Figure 8—Pulpwood production in the South, 1953–2010.

has made-up an increasingly larger share of total pulpwood production. Softwood roundwood was up 8 percent in 2010, accounting for 57 percent of total pulpwood production.

In contrast, hardwood roundwood as a proportion of total pulpwood production was only 12 percent in 1953 and steadily increased until 1997 when it accounted for 27 percent of total production. Since then the hardwood roundwood component has steadily declined. In 2010, with a 13-percent increase in hardwood roundwood production recorded it only accounted for 21 percent of total pulpwood production.

The production and use of wood residues in the South has taken much the same track as hardwood production. In 1953, wood residue was not recorded as being used for pulpwood production. The production and use of wood residue increased steadily until 1985 when it accounted for 35 percent of total pulpwood production. Since then the proportion of wood residue has declined. Although wood residues are still an important source of fiber for the pulp and paper industry in the South, the 1-percent decline in wood residue production in 2010 has reduced the proportion of wood residues to 22 percent of total pulpwood production.

Appendix

Table A.1—Pulpwood production in the Southeast and South Central regions, 2010

Region and source of wood	All species	Softwood	Hardwood	All species	Softwood	Hardwood
		standard cords			*green tons*	
Southeast[a]						
Roundwood	23,643,546	18,404,844	5,238,702	64,361,445	49,693,078	14,668,367
Residues	7,217,600	5,484,801	1,732,799	17,462,296	13,190,946	4,271,350
Total	30,861,146	23,889,645	6,971,501	81,823,741	62,884,024	18,939,717
South Central[b]						
Roundwood	27,342,735	18,681,970	8,660,765	74,691,463	50,441,321	24,250,142
Residues	7,338,957	5,673,679	1,665,278	17,750,107	13,645,198	4,104,909
Total	34,681,692	24,355,649	10,326,043	92,441,570	64,086,519	28,355,051
Entire South						
Roundwood	50,986,281	37,086,814	13,899,467	139,052,908	100,134,399	38,918,509
Residues	14,556,557	11,158,480	3,398,077	35,212,403	26,836,144	8,376,259
Total	65,542,838	48,245,294	17,297,544	174,265,311	126,970,543	47,294,768

[a] States of Florida, Georgia, North Carolina, South Carolina, and Virginia.
[b] States of Alabama, Arkansas, Kentucky, Louisiana, Mississippi, Oklahoma, Tennessee, and Texas.

Table A.2—Pulpwood production in the South by State and species group, 2010

State	Change	All species	Softwood	Hardwood	All species	Softwood	Hardwood
	percent	- - - - - - - - *standard cords* - - - - - - - -				*green tons*	
Alabama	8	10,167,833	7,344,468	2,823,365	27,068,763	19,295,706	7,773,057
Arkansas	13	4,317,389	2,938,430	1,378,959	11,480,925	7,662,738	3,818,187
Florida	-3	4,484,484	4,227,802	256,682	11,841,495	11,134,006	707,489
Georgia	14	11,429,219	9,483,255	1,945,964	30,407,575	25,087,660	5,319,915
Kentucky	3	589,505	41,138	548,367	1,577,829	110,778	1,467,051
Louisiana	3	5,902,359	4,933,609	968,750	15,683,755	13,014,703	2,669,052
Mississippi	16	7,596,666	5,737,796	1,858,870	20,308,620	15,206,348	5,102,272
North Carolina	6	5,146,392	3,340,715	1,805,677	13,556,989	8,740,380	4,816,609
Oklahoma	10	583,664	330,618	253,046	1,599,001	890,829	708,172
South Carolina	-4	6,186,448	4,865,156	1,321,292	16,393,671	12,755,041	3,638,630
Tennessee	13	1,960,502	574,309	1,386,193	5,342,312	1,544,701	3,797,611
Texas	7	3,563,774	2,455,281	1,108,493	9,380,365	6,360,716	3,019,649
Virginia	2	3,614,603	1,972,717	1,641,886	9,624,011	5,166,937	4,457,074
All States	7	65,542,838	48,245,294	17,297,544	174,265,311	126,970,543	47,294,768

Table A.3—Roundwood production in the South by State and species group, 2010 and 2009

State	Change from 2009	2010			2009		
		All species	Softwood	Hardwood	All species	Softwood	Hardwood
	percent	- *thousand cords* -
Alabama	13	7,961.3	5,533.1	2,428.2	7,070.6	5,020.9	2,049.7
Arkansas	13	3,270.6	2,019.7	1,250.9	2,886.4	1,826.8	1,059.6
Florida	-5	3,498.2	3,275.1	223.2	3,670.1	3,456.1	214.0
Georgia	16	9,291.8	7,730.3	1,561.5	8,004.2	6,786.6	1,217.6
Kentucky	4	384.4	40.1	344.3	369.0	79.0	290.0
Louisiana	5	4,735.2	3,896.2	839.1	4,491.7	3,606.4	885.3
Mississippi	18	6,322.0	4,769.3	1,552.7	5,349.1	4,043.9	1,305.2
North Carolina	2	3,484.5	2,393.1	1,091.4	3,417.2	2,238.4	1,178.8
Oklahoma	15	576.4	324.4	252.0	503.4	274.2	229.2
South Carolina	-1	4,713.3	3,574.0	1,139.2	4,774.5	3,740.1	1,034.4
Tennessee	10	1,690.5	554.2	1,136.3	1,536.0	517.9	1,018.1
Texas	2	2,402.3	1,545.0	857.4	2,350.1	1,487.9	862.2
Virginia	27	2,655.8	1,432.4	1,223.4	2,094.7	1,149.9	944.8
All States	10	50,986.4	37,086.8	13,899.5	46,517.0	34,228.2	12,288.8

Numbers in rows may not sum to totals due to rounding.

Table A.4—Southern output of wood residues for pulp manufacture by State and species group, 2010 and 2009

State	Change from 2009	2010			2009		
		All species	Softwood	Hardwood	All species	Softwood	Hardwood
	percent	- *thousand cords* -
Alabama	-7	2,206.5	1,811.4	395.1	2,365.9	1,834.2	531.7
Arkansas	12	1,046.8	918.7	128.1	935.5	795.3	140.2
Florida	6	986.2	952.7	33.5	930.3	901.9	28.4
Georgia	6	2,137.4	1,753.0	384.4	2,025.3	1,665.4	359.9
Kentucky	0	205.1	1.0	204.1	205.9	1.9	204.0
Louisiana	-7	1,167.1	1,037.4	129.7	1,254.1	1,140.4	113.7
Mississippi	8	1,274.6	968.5	306.2	1,176.5	892.8	283.7
North Carolina	15	1,661.9	947.6	714.3	1,441.4	927.7	513.7
Oklahoma	-72	7.3	6.2	1.1	26.2	20.9	5.3
South Carolina	-10	1,473.2	1,291.1	182.1	1,636.5	1,412.2	224.3
Tennessee	33	270.1	20.1	249.9	202.8	5.9	196.9
Texas	18	1,161.5	910.3	251.1	986.7	832.5	154.2
Virginia	-34	958.9	540.3	418.5	1,450.5	807.5	643.0
All States	-1	14,556.6	11,158.5	3,398.1	14,637.3	11,238.5	3,398.8

Numbers in rows may not sum to totals due to rounding.

Table A.5—Pulpwood production in the South by source of wood, State, year, and number of mills

Source of wood and State	Year										
	2000	2001	2002	2003	2004	2005	2006	2007	2008	2009	2010
	thousand green tons										
Roundwood											
Alabama	21,537	20,575	21,537	19,222	20,535	20,913	21,331	21,540	21,140	19,296	21,738
Arkansas	8,009	7,582	7,720	7,751	9,134	8,551	8,476	8,406	8,370	7,899	8,956
Florida	9,802	9,619	9,397	10,096	9,250	7,950	8,345	8,933	8,102	9,931	9,468
Georgia	20,433	18,218	18,875	20,786	20,558	19,656	21,250	22,353	25,110	21,733	25,244
Kentucky	637	556	637	715	681	891	882	901	940	1,025	1,072
Louisiana	11,467	10,748	9,934	11,317	11,998	12,601	12,702	13,048	12,866	12,216	12,869
Mississippi	12,936	11,637	10,578	11,150	14,320	13,525	13,710	14,806	14,260	14,573	17,225
North Carolina	9,065	8,688	8,486	9,415	9,982	9,830	9,302	10,177	9,924	9,344	9,517
Oklahoma	1,272	1,118	1,669	1,466	1,216	1,214	1,206	1,262	1,602	1,382	1,581
South Carolina	10,501	10,284	10,416	10,706	11,769	12,256	11,957	11,834	12,677	12,995	12,840
Tennessee	4,891	4,685	4,284	4,463	4,098	4,458	4,361	4,314	4,200	4,249	4,678
Texas	4,195	5,843	5,720	7,124	7,327	7,179	6,202	6,473	7,614	6,432	6,572
Virginia	6,571	6,176	5,756	6,764	7,425	7,255	6,852	5,849	6,271	5,750	7,293
All States	121,316	115,729	115,009	120,974	128,292	126,280	126,575	129,897	133,075	126,825	139,053
Residues	53,898	51,340	52,603	41,039	40,711	42,982	44,367	43,936	44,075	35,407	35,212
Total	175,214	167,069	167,612	162,012	169,003	169,262	170,943	173,833	177,151	162,231	174,265
Number of mills	98	94	92	91	89	87	87	87	86	83	82

Numbers in columns may not sum to totals due to rounding.

Table A.6—Roundwood pulpwood production in Alabama, 2010

County[a]	All species	Softwood	Hardwood	All species	Softwood	Hardwood
	standard cords			*green tons*		
Autauga	80,876	51,536	29,340	221,299	139,147	82,152
Baldwin	190,766	164,802	25,964	517,664	444,965	72,699
Barbour	162,161	131,655	30,506	440,886	355,469	85,417
Bibb	100,244	66,660	33,584	274,017	179,982	94,035
Blount	46,158	6,520	39,638	128,590	17,604	110,986
Bullock	139,117	123,805	15,312	377,148	334,274	42,874
Butler	220,417	176,770	43,647	599,491	477,279	122,212
Calhoun	36,613	31,765	4,848	99,340	85,766	13,574
Chambers	98,935	77,564	21,371	269,262	209,423	59,839
Cherokee	122,107	100,901	21,206	331,810	272,433	59,377
Chilton	100,869	61,884	38,985	276,245	167,087	109,158
Choctaw	374,735	249,173	125,562	1,024,341	672,767	351,574
Clarke	475,167	309,698	165,469	1,299,498	836,185	463,313
Clay	149,843	111,860	37,983	408,374	302,022	106,352
Cleburne	101,902	92,823	9,079	276,043	250,622	25,421
Coffee	106,256	88,268	17,988	288,690	238,324	50,366
Colbert	42,921	23,059	19,862	117,873	62,259	55,614
Conecuh	238,867	198,892	39,975	648,938	537,008	111,930
Coosa	141,466	115,908	25,558	384,514	312,952	71,562
Covington	221,140	190,696	30,444	600,122	514,879	85,243
Crenshaw	212,860	159,104	53,756	580,098	429,581	150,517
Cullman	29,594	5,685	23,909	82,295	15,350	66,945
Dale	86,271	47,711	38,560	236,788	128,820	107,968
Dallas	175,052	111,540	63,512	478,992	301,158	177,834
De Kalb	32,235	18,746	13,489	88,383	50,614	37,769
Elmore	58,622	38,807	19,815	160,261	104,779	55,482
Escambia	151,161	115,202	35,959	411,730	311,045	100,685
Etowah	38,393	26,271	12,122	104,874	70,932	33,942
Fayette	61,070	35,783	25,287	167,418	96,614	70,804
Franklin	93,711	70,908	22,803	255,300	191,452	63,848
Geneva	90,186	79,063	11,123	244,614	213,470	31,144
Greene	75,601	35,707	39,894	208,112	96,409	111,703
Hale	73,645	36,355	37,290	202,571	98,159	104,412
Henry	107,384	72,911	34,473	293,384	196,860	96,524
Houston	38,705	20,621	18,084	106,312	55,677	50,635
Jackson	64,440	11,174	53,266	179,315	30,170	149,145
Jefferson	21,208	4,604	16,604	58,922	12,431	46,491
Lamar	96,138	49,318	46,820	264,255	133,159	131,096
Lauderdale	46,438	14,529	31,909	128,573	39,228	89,345
Lawrence	26,608	9,608	17,000	73,542	25,942	47,600
Lee	81,106	58,236	22,870	221,273	157,237	64,036
Limestone	5,883	1,662	4,221	16,306	4,487	11,819
Lowndes	149,946	107,596	42,350	409,089	290,509	118,580
Macon	113,242	84,725	28,517	308,606	228,758	79,848
Madison	12,859	5,012	7,847	35,504	13,532	21,972
Marengo	289,227	184,181	105,046	791,418	497,289	294,129
Marion	116,904	73,301	43,603	320,001	197,913	122,088
Marshall	10,667	1,031	9,636	29,765	2,784	26,981
Mobile	90,893	67,015	23,878	247,799	180,941	66,858
Monroe	294,724	217,157	77,567	803,512	586,324	217,188
Montgomery	86,759	57,370	29,389	237,188	154,899	82,289

continued

Table A.6—Roundwood pulpwood production in Alabama, 2010 (continued)

County[a]	All species	Softwood	Hardwood	All species	Softwood	Hardwood
	standard cords			green tons		
Morgan	31,065	6,401	24,664	86,342	17,283	69,059
Perry	157,053	110,400	46,653	428,708	298,080	130,628
Pickens	110,139	76,938	33,201	300,696	207,733	92,963
Pike	137,182	93,974	43,208	374,712	253,730	120,982
Randolph	115,382	96,911	18,471	313,379	261,660	51,719
Russell	71,600	55,395	16,205	194,941	149,567	45,374
St. Clair	82,394	44,574	37,820	226,246	120,350	105,896
Shelby	95,236	72,403	22,833	259,420	195,488	63,932
Sumter	179,952	124,541	55,411	491,412	336,261	155,151
Talladega	104,697	88,738	15,959	284,278	239,593	44,685
Tallapoosa	185,446	138,292	47,154	505,419	373,388	132,031
Tuscaloosa	121,117	47,739	73,378	334,353	128,895	205,458
Walker	24,629	12,211	12,418	67,740	32,970	34,770
Washington	249,375	149,689	99,686	683,281	404,160	279,121
Wilcox	253,100	180,323	72,777	690,648	486,872	203,776
Winston	60,876	39,386	21,490	166,514	106,342	60,172
All counties	7,961,335	5,533,087	2,428,248	21,738,434	14,939,342	6,799,092

[a] Counties with no pulpwood production are omitted.

Table A.7—Roundwood pulpwood production in Arkansas, 2010

County[a]	All species	Softwood	Hardwood	All species	Softwood	Hardwood
	standard cords			green tons		
Arkansas	19,862	5,639	14,223	55,049	15,225	39,824
Ashley	207,705	144,028	63,677	567,172	388,876	178,296
Baxter	1,320	9	1,311	3,695	24	3,671
Boone	2,787	0	2,787	7,804	0	7,804
Bradley	179,002	137,107	41,895	487,495	370,189	117,306
Calhoun	63,624	47,191	16,433	173,428	127,416	46,012
Chicot	32,945	2,553	30,392	91,991	6,893	85,098
Clark	172,340	66,790	105,550	475,873	180,333	295,540
Clay	63	63	0	170	170	0
Cleburne	30,888	25,238	5,650	83,963	68,143	15,820
Cleveland	113,043	61,096	51,947	310,411	164,959	145,452
Columbia	34,089	10,283	23,806	94,421	27,764	66,657
Conway	25,351	22,745	2,606	68,709	61,412	7,297
Craighead	280	0	280	784	0	784
Crawford	10	0	10	28	0	28
Crittenden	102	0	102	286	0	286
Cross	5,572	184	5,388	15,583	497	15,086
Dallas	108,525	60,714	47,811	297,799	163,928	133,871
Desha	27,348	215	27,133	76,553	581	75,972
Drew	186,750	142,678	44,072	508,633	385,231	123,402
Faulkner	15,637	12,733	2,904	42,510	34,379	8,131
Franklin	1,058	1,012	46	2,861	2,732	129
Fulton	9	0	9	25	0	25
Garland	15,821	9,314	6,507	43,368	25,148	18,220
Grant	152,606	119,073	33,533	415,389	321,497	93,892

continued

Table A.7—Roundwood pulpwood production in Arkansas, 2010 (continued)

County[a]	All species	Softwood	Hardwood	All species	Softwood	Hardwood
	standard cords			*green tons*		
Greene	1,131	153	978	3,151	413	2,738
Hempstead	86,176	46,920	39,256	236,601	126,684	109,917
Hot Spring	90,301	72,775	17,526	245,566	196,493	49,073
Howard	95,207	61,514	33,693	260,428	166,088	94,340
Independence	34,039	11,453	22,586	94,164	30,923	63,241
Izard	7,296	1,590	5,706	20,270	4,293	15,977
Jackson	1,764	612	1,152	4,878	1,652	3,226
Jefferson	64,836	47,793	17,043	176,761	129,041	47,720
Johnson	32,341	11,164	21,177	89,439	30,143	59,296
Lafayette	81,452	53,121	28,331	222,754	143,427	79,327
Lawrence	454	0	454	1,271	0	1,271
Lee	2,551	0	2,551	7,143	0	7,143
Lincoln	80,686	36,460	44,226	222,275	98,442	123,833
Little River	135,496	92,010	43,486	370,188	248,427	121,761
Logan	9,891	6,704	3,187	27,025	18,101	8,924
Lonoke	10,334	7,535	2,799	28,182	20,345	7,837
Madison	7,293	600	6,693	20,360	1,620	18,740
Marion	8,739	333	8,406	24,436	899	23,537
Miller	39,600	12,798	26,802	109,601	34,555	75,046
Mississippi	567	0	567	1,588	0	1,588
Monroe	4,840	915	3,925	13,461	2,471	10,990
Montgomery	17,674	12,350	5,324	48,252	33,345	14,907
Nevada	76,659	44,354	32,305	210,210	119,756	90,454
Newton	475	72	403	1,322	194	1,128
Ouachita	75,529	33,946	41,583	208,086	91,654	116,432
Perry	36,710	33,588	3,122	99,430	90,688	8,742
Phillips	3,651	0	3,651	10,223	0	10,223
Pike	106,667	86,974	19,693	289,970	234,830	55,140
Poinsett	10	0	10	28	0	28
Polk	62,509	46,106	16,403	170,414	124,486	45,928
Pope	29,013	19,718	9,295	79,265	53,239	26,026
Prairie	13,471	9,811	3,660	36,738	26,490	10,248
Pulaski	12,765	6,830	5,935	35,059	18,441	16,618
Randolph	65	0	65	182	0	182
St. Francis	5,641	11	5,630	15,794	30	15,764
Saline	45,717	29,817	15,900	125,026	80,506	44,520
Scott	52,910	36,873	16,037	144,461	99,557	44,904
Searcy	12,971	2,771	10,200	36,042	7,482	28,560
Sebastian	775	775	0	2,093	2,093	0
Sevier	96,867	62,396	34,471	264,988	168,469	96,519
Sharp	8,073	3,571	4,502	22,248	9,642	12,606
Stone	19,104	4,627	14,477	53,029	12,493	40,536
Union	163,186	104,869	58,317	446,434	283,146	163,288
Van Buren	71,103	25,646	45,457	196,524	69,244	127,280
Washington	4,954	0	4,954	13,871	0	13,871
White	104,581	86,498	18,083	284,177	233,545	50,632
Woodruff	864	0	864	2,419	0	2,419
Yell	56,935	34,987	21,948	155,919	94,465	61,454
All counties	3,270,610	2,019,705	1,250,905	8,955,746	5,453,209	3,502,537

[a] Counties with no pulpwood production are omitted.

Table A.8—Roundwood pulpwood production in Florida, 2010

County[a]	All species	Softwood	Hardwood	All species	Softwood	Hardwood
	standard cords			*green tons*		
Alachua	72,161	68,355	3,806	195,216	184,559	10,657
Baker	155,630	145,414	10,216	421,223	392,618	28,605
Bay	1,865	1,331	534	5,089	3,594	1,495
Bradford	35,552	31,074	4,478	96,438	83,900	12,538
Brevard	304	138	166	838	373	465
Calhoun	125,390	115,403	9,987	339,552	311,588	27,964
Charlotte	320	320	0	864	864	0
Citrus	966	13	953	2,703	35	2,668
Clay	224,401	223,406	995	605,982	603,196	2,786
Columbia	72,194	70,110	2,084	195,132	189,297	5,835
Dixie	113,803	103,411	10,392	308,308	279,210	29,098
Duval	71,005	67,994	3,011	192,015	183,584	8,431
Escambia	34,090	31,644	2,446	92,288	85,439	6,849
Flagler	122,779	110,603	12,176	332,721	298,628	34,093
Franklin	113	103	10	306	278	28
Gadsden	43,773	31,261	12,512	119,439	84,405	35,034
Gilchrist	39,881	37,877	2,004	107,879	102,268	5,611
Gulf	164,312	163,779	533	443,695	442,203	1,492
Hamilton	123,427	119,213	4,214	333,674	321,875	11,799
Hernando	980	23	957	2,742	62	2,680
Highlands	64	0	64	179	0	179
Hillsborough	54	0	54	151	0	151
Holmes	69,418	60,678	8,740	188,303	163,831	24,472
Jackson	59,386	40,921	18,465	162,189	110,487	51,702
Jefferson	27,649	24,111	3,538	75,006	65,100	9,906
Lafayette	154,887	149,272	5,615	418,756	403,034	15,722
Lake	3,531	3,174	357	9,570	8,570	1,000
Leon	23,855	22,555	1,300	64,539	60,899	3,640
Levy	132,790	111,946	20,844	360,617	302,254	58,363
Liberty	92,646	89,040	3,606	250,505	240,408	10,097
Madison	152,620	150,891	1,729	412,247	407,406	4,841
Marion	64,688	56,072	8,616	175,519	151,394	24,125
Martin	10	10	0	27	27	0
Monroe	21	21	0	57	57	0
Nassau	269,540	265,724	3,816	728,140	717,455	10,685
Okaloosa	56,976	53,415	3,561	154,192	144,221	9,971
Orange	468	442	26	1,266	1,193	73
Pasco	124	4	120	347	11	336
Polk	93	34	59	257	92	165
Putnam	83,678	68,325	15,353	227,466	184,478	42,988
St. Johns	112,382	100,692	11,690	304,600	271,868	32,732
St. Lucie	13	5	8	36	14	22
Santa Rosa	85,817	79,072	6,745	232,380	213,494	18,886
Seminole	92	18	74	256	49	207
Sumter	3,007	727	2,280	8,347	1,963	6,384
Suwannee	191,851	190,642	1,209	518,118	514,733	3,385
Taylor	277,433	275,670	1,763	749,245	744,309	4,936
Union	14,133	9,621	4,512	38,611	25,977	12,634
Volusia	34,131	31,007	3,124	92,466	83,719	8,747
Wakulla	6,190	5,072	1,118	16,824	13,694	3,130
Walton	117,198	111,052	6,146	317,049	299,840	17,209
Washington	60,555	53,374	7,181	164,217	144,110	20,107
All counties	3,498,246	3,275,059	223,187	9,467,586	8,842,663	624,923

[a] Counties with no pulpwood production are omitted.

Table A.9—Roundwood pulpwood production in Georgia, 2010

County[a]	All species	Softwood	Hardwood	All species	Softwood	Hardwood
		standard cords			*green tons*	
Appling	157,990	138,579	19,411	428,514	374,163	54,351
Atkinson	51,684	39,066	12,618	140,808	105,478	35,330
Bacon	119,023	109,069	9,954	322,357	294,486	27,871
Baker	14,597	14,198	399	39,452	38,335	1,117
Baldwin	30,226	21,565	8,661	82,477	58,226	24,251
Banks	10,578	3,838	6,740	29,235	10,363	18,872
Barrow	1,378	668	710	3,792	1,804	1,988
Bartow	113,803	98,722	15,081	308,776	266,549	42,227
Ben Hill	15,662	15,075	587	42,347	40,703	1,644
Berrien	31,396	21,820	9,576	85,727	58,914	26,813
Bibb	20,246	10,251	9,995	55,664	27,678	27,986
Bleckley	35,623	27,126	8,497	97,032	73,240	23,792
Brantley	139,274	128,816	10,458	377,085	347,803	29,282
Brooks	19,598	18,295	1,303	53,045	49,397	3,648
Bryan	97,812	86,225	11,587	265,252	232,808	32,444
Bulloch	107,718	89,765	17,953	292,634	242,366	50,268
Burke	235,683	179,059	56,624	642,006	483,459	158,547
Butts	14,667	11,384	3,283	39,929	30,737	9,192
Calhoun	33,563	32,742	821	90,702	88,403	2,299
Camden	173,828	162,449	11,379	470,473	438,612	31,861
Candler	43,931	40,382	3,549	118,968	109,031	9,937
Carroll	115,970	112,386	3,584	313,477	303,442	10,035
Catoosa	2,603	1,210	1,393	7,167	3,267	3,900
Charlton	341,769	336,426	5,343	923,310	908,350	14,960
Chatham	32,437	29,041	3,396	87,920	78,411	9,509
Chattahoochee	38,878	26,055	12,823	106,253	70,349	35,904
Chattooga	57,122	35,948	21,174	156,347	97,060	59,287
Cherokee	47,434	39,769	7,665	128,838	107,376	21,462
Clarke	694	182	512	1,925	491	1,434
Clay	28,057	23,110	4,947	76,249	62,397	13,852
Clayton	2,944	2,700	244	7,973	7,290	683
Clinch	231,029	181,190	49,839	628,762	489,213	139,549
Cobb	1,727	1,627	100	4,673	4,393	280
Coffee	71,498	66,605	4,893	193,534	179,834	13,700
Colquitt	20,096	17,280	2,816	54,541	46,656	7,885
Columbia	22,332	12,678	9,654	61,262	34,231	27,031
Cook	12,053	9,193	2,860	32,829	24,821	8,008
Coweta	36,208	33,296	2,912	98,053	89,899	8,154
Crawford	92,340	87,715	4,625	249,781	236,831	12,950
Crisp	13,218	8,794	4,424	36,131	23,744	12,387
Dade	5,916	2,076	3,840	16,357	5,605	10,752
Dawson	32,334	27,461	4,873	87,789	74,145	13,644
Decatur	51,185	41,539	9,646	139,164	112,155	27,009
De Kalb	422	366	56	1,145	988	157
Dodge	87,182	67,405	19,777	237,370	181,994	55,376
Dooly	36,511	27,479	9,032	99,483	74,193	25,290
Dougherty	38,432	31,612	6,820	104,448	85,352	19,096
Douglas	10,683	8,483	2,200	29,064	22,904	6,160
Early	80,039	68,744	11,295	217,235	185,609	31,626
Echols	34,994	26,600	8,394	95,323	71,820	23,503
Effingham	111,027	85,391	25,636	302,337	230,556	71,781
Elbert	23,821	11,629	12,192	65,536	31,398	34,138
Emanuel	178,169	154,122	24,047	483,461	416,129	67,332
Evans	48,261	43,941	4,320	130,737	118,641	12,096

continued

Table A.9—Roundwood pulpwood production in Georgia, 2010 (continued)

County[a]	All species	Softwood	Hardwood	All species	Softwood	Hardwood
	standard cords			*green tons*		
Fannin	3,982	3,509	473	10,798	9,474	1,324
Fayette	1,159	290	869	3,216	783	2,433
Floyd	183,056	159,209	23,847	496,636	429,864	66,772
Forsyth	6,808	3,972	2,836	18,665	10,724	7,941
Franklin	15,135	6,044	9,091	41,774	16,319	25,455
Fulton	11,644	8,994	2,650	31,704	24,284	7,420
Gilmer	19,553	14,233	5,320	53,325	38,429	14,896
Glascock	49,681	38,932	10,749	135,213	105,116	30,097
Glynn	68,125	63,852	,273	184,364	172,400	11,964
Gordon	48,925	35,794	13,131	133,411	96,644	36,767
Grady	169,092	158,073	11,019	457,650	426,797	30,853
Greene	54,779	37,457	17,322	149,636	101,134	48,502
Gwinnett	12,284	7,792	4,492	33,616	21,038	12,578
Habersham	2,471	1,511	960	6,768	4,080	2,688
Hall	9,203	3,047	6,156	25,464	8,227	17,237
Hancock	97,897	81,222	16,675	265,989	219,299	46,690
Haralson	82,695	73,158	9,537	224,231	197,527	26,704
Harris	67,320	57,732	9,588	182,722	155,876	26,846
Hart	8,244	2,671	5,573	22,816	7,212	15,604
Heard	93,701	86,389	7,312	253,724	233,250	20,474
Henry	21,275	11,336	9,939	58,436	30,607	27,829
Houston	47,396	39,077	8,319	128,801	105,508	23,293
Irwin	19,493	13,993	5,500	53,181	37,781	15,400
Jackson	20,507	5,239	15,268	56,895	14,145	42,750
Jasper	55,875	36,168	19,707	152,834	97,654	55,180
Jeff Davis	86,691	78,740	7,951	234,861	212,598	22,263
Jefferson	137,470	110,224	27,246	373,894	297,605	76,289
Jenkins	79,848	67,967	11,881	216,778	183,511	33,267
Johnson	81,810	59,221	22,589	223,146	159,897	63,249
Jones	53,547	41,758	11,789	145,756	112,747	33,009
Lamar	36,011	15,953	20,058	99,235	43,073	56,162
Lanier	21,356	20,284	1,072	57,769	54,767	3,002
Laurens	200,710	157,761	42,949	546,212	425,955	120,257
Lee	36,972	30,807	6,165	100,441	83,179	17,262
Liberty	77,497	68,713	8,784	210,120	185,525	24,595
Lincoln	13,443	7,958	5,485	36,845	21,487	15,358
Long	155,614	149,485	6,129	420,771	403,610	17,161
Lowndes	32,463	26,216	6,247	88,275	70,783	17,492
Lumpkin	2,958	1,926	1,032	8,090	5,200	2,890
Macon	83,887	74,198	9,689	227,464	200,335	27,129
Madison	6,230	1,354	4,876	17,309	3,656	13,653
Marion	96,290	92,967	3,323	260,315	251,011	9,304
McDuffie	45,047	34,114	10,933	122,720	92,108	30,612
McIntosh	116,754	105,699	11,055	316,341	285,387	30,954
Meriwether	69,989	54,713	15,276	190,498	147,725	42,773
Miller	14,268	7,081	7,187	39,243	19,119	20,124
Mitchell	51,278	46,347	4,931	138,944	125,137	13,807
Monroe	67,091	51,998	15,093	182,655	140,395	42,260
Montgomery	89,696	73,209	16,487	243,828	197,664	46,164
Morgan	36,305	25,299	11,006	99,124	68,307	30,817
Murray	62,216	43,789	18,427	169,826	118,230	51,596
Muscogee	1,451	700	751	3,993	1,890	2,103
Newton	19,222	15,984	3,238	52,223	43,157	9,066
Oconee	5,951	3,497	2,454	16,313	9,442	6,871

continued

Table A.9—Roundwood pulpwood production in Georgia, 2010 (continued)

County[a]	All species	Softwood	Hardwood	All species	Softwood	Hardwood
	standard cords			*green tons*		
Oglethorpe	34,557	19,550	15,007	94,805	52,785	42,020
Paulding	69,086	49,431	19,655	188,498	133,464	55,034
Peach	7,399	6,818	581	20,036	18,409	1,627
Pickens	21,344	19,097	2,247	57,854	51,562	6,292
Pierce	100,349	77,239	23,110	273,253	208,545	64,708
Pike	28,461	27,082	1,379	76,982	73,121	3,861
Polk	73,304	53,848	19,456	199,867	145,390	54,477
Pulaski	35,317	29,735	5,582	95,915	80,285	15,630
Putnam	46,707	36,762	9,945	127,103	99,257	27,846
Quitman	39,909	27,779	12,130	108,967	75,003	33,964
Rabun	1,915	379	1,536	5,324	1,023	4,301
Randolph	94,902	81,720	13,182	257,554	220,644	36,910
Richmond	31,512	19,746	11,766	86,259	53,314	32,945
Rockdale	4,712	4,461	251	12,748	12,045	703
Schley	55,889	54,272	1,617	151,062	146,534	4,528
Screven	196,825	148,640	48,185	536,246	401,328	134,918
Seminole	16,449	14,560	1,889	44,601	39,312	5,289
Spalding	4,262	3,737	525	11,560	10,090	1,470
Stephens	2,636	612	2,024	7,319	1,652	5,667
Stewart	134,272	127,644	6,628	363,197	344,639	18,558
Sumter	77,823	75,309	2,514	210,373	203,334	7,039
Talbot	75,108	64,162	10,946	203,886	173,237	30,649
Taliaferro	18,699	11,905	6,794	51,167	32,144	19,023
Tattnall	127,848	119,784	8,064	345,996	323,417	22,579
Taylor	73,715	69,331	4,384	199,469	187,194	12,275
Telfair	78,259	65,449	12,810	212,580	176,712	35,868
Terrell	33,788	33,044	744	91,302	89,219	2,083
Thomas	55,555	47,509	8,046	150,803	128,274	22,529
Tift	7,830	1,829	6,001	21,741	4,938	16,803
Toombs	105,977	88,501	17,476	287,886	238,953	48,933
Towns	1,088	0	1,088	3,046	0	3,046
Treutlen	41,354	32,629	8,725	112,528	88,098	24,430
Troup	96,843	62,486	34,357	264,912	168,712	96,200
Turner	19,440	16,487	2,953	52,783	44,515	8,268
Twiggs	92,171	69,695	22,476	251,110	188,177	62,933
Union	4,929	4,371	558	13,364	11,802	1,562
Upson	49,450	37,995	11,455	134,661	102,587	32,074
Walker	21,718	14,543	7,175	59,356	39,266	20,090
Walton	11,359	6,381	4,978	31,167	17,229	13,938
Ware	139,867	123,814	16,053	379,246	334,298	44,948
Warren	69,210	49,430	19,780	188,845	133,461	55,384
Washington	206,434	173,043	33,391	560,711	467,216	93,495
Wayne	204,921	190,078	14,843	554,771	513,211	41,560
Webster	33,812	29,820	3,992	91,692	80,514	11,178
Wheeler	93,855	80,780	13,075	254,716	218,106	36,610
White	2,858	1,842	1,016	7,818	4,973	2,845
Whitfield	43,344	41,743	1,601	117,189	112,706	4,483
Wilcox	26,730	20,312	6,418	72,812	54,842	17,970
Wilkes	48,439	30,306	18,133	132,598	81,826	50,772
Wilkinson	64,475	42,671	21,804	176,263	115,212	61,051
Worth	37,075	33,115	3,960	100,499	89,411	11,088
All counties	9,291,811	7,730,279	1,561,532	25,244,047	20,871,757	4,372,290

[a] Counties with no pulpwood production are omitted.

Table A.10—Roundwood pulpwood production in Kentucky, 2010

County[a]	All species	Softwood	Hardwood	All species	Softwood	Hardwood
	standard cords			*green tons*		
Ballard	6,448	1,022	5,426	17,952	2,759	15,193
Breathitt	26	0	26	73	0	73
Breckinridge	16,292	21	16,271	45,616	57	45,559
Butler	3,525	0	3,525	9,870	0	9,870
Caldwell	9,430	3,867	5,563	26,017	10,441	15,576
Calloway	1,572	1,572	0	4,244	4,244	0
Carlisle	2,022	121	1,901	5,650	327	5,323
Carter	68	24	44	188	65	123
Christian	7,714	6,567	1,147	20,943	17,731	3,212
Crittenden	8,035	638	7,397	22,435	1,723	20,712
Daviess	1,221	1,037	184	3,315	2,800	515
Edmonson	2,517	0	2,517	7,048	0	7,048
Fulton	775	0	775	2,170	0	2,170
Graves	14,160	91	14,069	39,639	246	39,393
Grayson	12,476	39	12,437	34,929	105	34,824
Greenup	68,262	965	67,297	191,038	2,606	188,432
Hancock	937	933	4	2,530	2,519	11
Hardin	1,171	1,171	0	3,162	3,162	0
Harlan	595	0	595	1,666	0	1,666
Hickman	426	0	426	1,193	0	1,193
Hopkins	1,875	1,147	728	5,135	3,097	2,038
Jefferson	40	40	0	108	108	0
Knox	37,350	9	37,341	104,579	24	104,555
Laurel	53,035	747	52,288	148,423	2,017	146,406
Lawrence	179	0	179	501	0	501
Letcher	397	0	397	1,112	0	1,112
Lewis	12,552	177	12,375	35,128	478	34,650
Livingston	13,191	11,262	1,929	35,808	30,407	5,401
Logan	315	0	315	882	0	882
Lyon	7,630	16	7,614	21,362	43	21,319
Marshall	5,411	39	5,372	15,147	105	15,042
McCreary	18,529	825	17,704	51,799	2,228	49,571
McLean	932	147	785	2,595	397	2,198
Metcalfe	52	0	52	146	0	146
Muhlenberg	1,067	309	758	2,956	834	2,122
Ohio	57,878	1,920	55,958	161,866	5,184	156,682
Rowan	629	14	615	1,760	38	1,722
Trigg	8,296	4,470	3,826	22,782	12,069	10,713
Union	412	0	412	1,154	0	1,154
Warren	563	0	563	1,576	0	1,576
Whitley	6,392	948	5,444	17,803	2,560	15,243
All counties	384,397	40,138	344,259	1,072,300	108,374	963,926

[a] Counties with no pulpwood production are omitted.

Table A.11—Roundwood pulpwood production in Louisiana, 2010

Parish[a]	All species	Softwood	Hardwood	All species	Softwood	Hardwood
	standard cords			green tons		
Acadia	911	741	170	2,477	2,001	476
Allen	195,859	164,568	31,291	531,949	444,334	87,615
Ascension	2,420	825	1,595	6,694	2,228	4,466
Assumption	156	0	156	437	0	437
Avoyelles	4,360	3,131	1,229	11,895	8,454	3,441
Beauregard	394,200	367,799	26,401	1,066,980	993,057	73,923
Bienville	214,191	199,187	15,004	579,816	537,805	42,011
Bossier	123,409	67,772	55,637	338,768	182,984	155,784
Caddo	56,623	34,298	22,325	155,115	92,605	62,510
Calcasieu	45,968	45,968	0	124,114	124,114	0
Caldwell	132,035	120,530	11,505	357,645	325,431	32,214
Cameron	5,434	224	5,210	15,193	605	14,588
Catahoula	17,868	14,665	3,203	48,564	39,596	8,968
Claiborne	142,314	109,054	33,260	387,574	294,446	93,128
Concordia	10,531	78	10,453	29,479	211	29,268
De Soto	251,567	207,852	43,715	683,602	561,200	122,402
East Baton Rouge	18,488	8,768	9,720	50,890	23,674	27,216
East Carroll	14,229	41	14,188	39,837	111	9,726
East Feliciana	77,888	50,510	27,378	213,035	136,377	76,658
Evangeline	21,587	16,187	5,400	58,825	43,705	15,120
Franklin	16,525	11,195	5,330	45,151	30,227	14,924
Grant	113,865	99,427	14,438	308,879	268,453	40,426
Iberia	40	0	40	112	0	112
Iberville	12,617	31	12,586	35,325	84	35,241
Jackson	216,997	211,740	5,257	586,418	571,698	14,720
Jefferson	21	0	21	59	0	59
Jefferson Davis	5,612	3,397	2,215	15,374	9,172	6,202
La Salle	191,195	173,566	17,629	517,989	468,628	49,361
Lafayette	84	11	73	234	30	204
Lafourche	9,447	0	9,447	26,452	0	26,452
Lincoln	87,729	79,950	7,779	237,646	215,865	21,781
Livingston	55,791	35,982	19,809	152,616	97,151	55,465
Madison	9,777	10	9,767	27,375	27	27,348
Morehouse	44,540	36,672	7,868	121,044	99,014	22,030
Natchitoches	127,537	94,462	33,075	347,657	255,047	92,610
Ouachita	70,269	63,096	7,173	190,443	170,359	20,084
Plaquemines	13	13	0	35	35	0
Pointe Coupee	23,976	12	23,964	67,131	32	67,099
Rapides	138,266	103,018	35,248	376,843	278,149	98,694
Red River	78,613	63,020	15,593	213,814	170,154	43,660
Richland	2,998	969	2,029	8,297	2,616	5,681
Sabine	264,090	237,283	26,807	715,724	640,664	75,060
St. Charles	32	21	11	88	57	31
St. Helena	98,257	79,715	18,542	267,149	215,231	51,918
St. James	2,451	22	2,429	6,860	59	6,801
St. Landry	24,103	5,307	18,796	66,958	14,329	52,629
St. Martin	1,444	12	1,432	4,042	32	4,010
St. Mary	184	12	172	514	32	482
St. Tammany	54,609	54,496	113	147,455	147,139	316
Tangipahoa	188,218	158,337	29,881	511,177	427,510	83,667
Tensas	9,126	21	9,105	25,551	57	25,494
Terrebonne	866	76	790	2,417	205	2,212

continued

Table A.11—Roundwood pulpwood production in Louisiana, 2010 (continued)

Parish[a]	All species	Softwood	Hardwood	All species	Softwood	Hardwood
	standard cords			*green tons*		
Union	245,063	163,417	81,646	669,835	441,226	228,609
Vernon	408,558	367,234	41,324	1,107,239	991,532	115,707
Washington	133,539	131,671	1,868	360,742	355,512	5,230
Webster	34,837	12,721	22,116	96,272	34,347	61,925
West Baton Rouge	18	0	18	50	0	50
West Carroll	5,444	4,494	950	14,794	12,134	2,660
West Feliciana	29,632	17,138	12,494	81,256	46,273	34,983
Winn	298,811	275,434	23,377	809,128	743,672	65,456
All parishes	4,735,232	3,896,180	839,052	12,869,034	10,519,690	2,349,344

[a] Parishes with no pulpwood production are omitted.

Table A.12—Roundwood pulpwood production in Mississippi, 2010

County[a]	All species	Softwood	Hardwood	All species	Softwood	Hardwood
	standard cords			*green tons*		
Adams	18,012	2,849	15,163	50,148	7,692	42,456
Alcorn	28,246	21,287	6,959	76,960	57,475	19,485
Amite	121,416	100,586	20,830	329,906	271,582	58,324
Attala	103,195	87,155	16,040	280,231	235,319	44,912
Benton	33,549	19,784	13,765	91,959	53,417	38,542
Bolivar	10,473	1,056	9,417	29,219	2,851	26,368
Calhoun	70,850	58,318	12,532	192,549	157,459	35,090
Carroll	103,887	83,546	20,341	282,529	225,574	56,955
Chickasaw	30,456	27,192	3,264	82,557	73,418	9,139
Choctaw	72,150	68,187	3,963	195,201	184,105	11,096
Claiborne	64,756	31,444	33,312	178,173	84,899	93,274
Clarke	174,604	148,242	26,362	474,067	400,253	73,814
Clay	32,482	21,512	10,970	88,798	58,082	30,716
Coahoma	2,946	33	2,913	8,245	89	8,156
Copiah	168,260	145,020	23,240	456,626	391,554	65,072
Covington	117,016	75,508	41,508	320,094	203,872	116,222
De Soto	11,267	10,433	834	30,504	28,169	2,335
Forrest	34,783	31,381	3,402	94,255	84,729	9,526
Franklin	124,601	68,589	56,012	342,024	185,190	156,834
George	63,507	61,704	1,803	171,649	166,601	5,048
Greene	170,220	147,370	22,850	461,879	397,899	63,980
Grenada	41,600	22,844	18,756	114,196	61,679	52,517
Hancock	40,521	40,521	0	109,407	109,407	0
Harrison	22,721	22,712	9	61,347	61,322	25
Hinds	95,905	71,574	24,331	261,377	193,250	68,127
Holmes	80,963	57,252	23,711	220,971	154,580	66,391
Humphreys	4,555	9	4,546	12,753	24	12,729
Issaquena	30,713	30	30,683	85,993	81	85,912
Itawamba	51,205	9,610	41,595	142,413	25,947	116,466
Jackson	41,567	41,567	0	112,231	112,231	0
Jasper	98,624	82,155	16,469	267,932	221,819	46,113
Jefferson	66,784	48,694	18,090	182,126	131,474	50,652

continued

Table A.12—Roundwood pulpwood production in Mississippi, 2010 (continued)

County[a]	All species	Softwood	Hardwood	All species	Softwood	Hardwood
	standard cords			green tons		
Jefferson Davis	61,772	61,510	262	166,811	166,077	734
Jones	146,791	110,487	36,304	399,966	298,315	101,651
Kemper	181,616	142,155	39,461	494,310	383,819	110,491
Lafayette	70,440	55,869	14,571	191,645	150,846	40,799
Lamar	63,554	63,323	231	171,619	170,972	647
Lauderdale	223,957	125,614	98,343	614,518	339,158	275,360
Lawrence	113,502	110,651	2,851	306,741	298,758	7,983
Leake	108,964	100,374	8,590	295,062	271,010	24,052
Lee	771	257	514	2,133	694	1,439
Leflore	11,287	41	11,246	31,600	111	31,489
Lincoln	306,190	219,130	87,060	835,419	591,651	243,768
Lowndes	34,361	25,046	9,315	93,706	67,624	26,082
Madison	94,171	81,460	12,711	255,533	219,942	35,591
Marion	271,709	222,133	49,576	738,572	599,759	138,813
Marshall	27,274	18,177	9,097	74,550	49,078	25,472
Monroe	68,300	27,898	40,402	188,451	75,325	113,126
Montgomery	88,868	55,834	33,034	243,247	150,752	92,495
Neshoba	94,593	73,528	21,065	257,508	198,526	58,982
Newton	86,853	74,305	12,548	235,758	200,624	35,134
Noxubee	121,410	104,896	16,514	329,458	283,219	46,239
Oktibbeha	42,056	36,730	5,326	114,084	99,171	14,913
Panola	45,700	32,601	13,099	124,700	88,023	36,677
Pearl River	85,030	76,865	8,165	230,398	207,536	22,862
Perry	129,327	122,136	7,191	349,902	329,767	20,135
Pike	28,383	27,428	955	76,730	74,056	2,674
Pontotoc	30,088	18,099	11,989	82,436	48,867	33,569
Prentiss	22,501	16,338	6,163	61,369	44,113	17,256
Quitman	27	0	27	76	0	76
Rankin	79,732	72,153	7,579	216,034	194,813	21,221
Scott	81,414	46,399	35,015	223,319	125,277	98,042
Sharkey	15,564	18	15,546	43,578	49	43,529
Simpson	122,613	84,841	37,772	334,833	229,071	105,762
Smith	206,756	204,778	1,978	558,439	552,901	5,538
Stone	58,410	58,194	216	157,729	157,124	605
Sunflower	808	8	800	2,262	22	2,240
Tallahatchie	18,081	11,916	6,165	49,435	32,173	17,262
Tate	4,839	3,327	1,512	13,217	8,983	4,234
Tippah	51,558	35,019	16,539	140,860	94,551	46,309
Tishomingo	109,423	46,160	63,263	301,768	124,632	177,136
Tunica	3,607	0	3,607	10,100	0	10,100
Union	31,580	19,263	12,317	86,498	52,010	34,488
Walthall	62,028	61,127	901	167,566	165,043	2,523
Warren	37,554	4,838	32,716	104,668	13,063	91,605
Washington	18,519	77	18,442	51,846	208	51,638
Wayne	187,414	144,564	42,850	510,303	390,323	119,980
Webster	78,694	71,282	7,412	213,215	192,461	20,754
Wilkinson	148,604	95,335	53,269	406,558	257,405	149,153
Winston	195,534	113,522	82,012	536,143	306,509	229,634
Yalobusha	72,746	63,791	8,955	197,310	172,236	25,074
Yazoo	45,220	21,656	23,564	124,450	58,471	65,979
All counties	6,322,027	4,769,317	1,552,710	17,224,752	12,877,161	4,347,591

[a] Counties with no pulpwood production are omitted.

Table A.13—Roundwood pulpwood production in North Carolina, 2010

County[a]	All species	Softwood	Hardwood	All species	Softwood	Hardwood
		standard cords			green tons	
Alamance	7,069	675	6,394	19,726	1,823	17,903
Alexander	1,245	47	1,198	3,481	127	3,354
Alleghany	7,541	41	7,500	21,111	111	21,000
Anson	77,224	69,917	7,307	209,236	188,776	20,460
Ashe	6,697	186	6,511	18,733	502	18,231
Avery	1,368	30	1,338	3,827	81	3,746
Beaufort	146,060	118,737	27,323	397,094	320,590	76,504
Bertie	113,604	105,398	8,206	307,552	284,575	22,977
Bladen	112,693	95,985	16,708	305,942	259,160	46,782
Brunswick	67,270	51,924	15,346	183,164	140,195	42,969
Buncombe	8,612	3,380	5,232	23,776	9,126	14,650
Burke	28,790	10,735	18,055	79,539	28,985	50,554
Cabarrus	5,197	4,927	270	14,059	13,303	756
Caldwell	4,583	336	4,247	12,799	907	11,892
Camden	22,485	13,001	9,484	61,658	35,103	26,555
Carteret	47,198	43,030	4,168	127,851	116,181	11,670
Caswell	18,305	1,592	16,713	51,094	4,298	46,796
Catawba	13,286	1,551	11,735	37,046	4,188	32,858
Chatham	2,249	861	1,388	6,211	2,325	3,886
Cherokee	26,925	8,061	18,864	74,584	21,765	52,819
Chowan	11,648	10,211	1,437	31,594	27,570	4,024
Clay	14,182	5,612	8,570	39,148	15,152	23,996
Cleveland	46,330	12,076	34,254	128,516	32,605	95,911
Columbus	90,999	66,483	24,516	248,149	179,504	68,645
Craven	97,157	63,504	33,653	265,689	171,461	94,228
Cumberland	69,099	56,674	12,425	187,810	153,020	34,790
Currituck	53,049	41,516	11,533	144,385	112,093	32,292
Dare	970	795	175	2,637	2,147	490
Davidson	3,715	321	3,394	10,370	867	9,503
Davie	4,008	651	3,357	11,158	1,758	9,400
Duplin	66,437	42,516	23,921	181,772	114,793	66,979
Durham	1,714	294	1,420	4,770	794	3,976
Edgecombe	55,559	41,516	11,533	144,385	112,093	32,292
Forsyth	8,606	1,208	7,398	23,976	3,262	20,714
Franklin	53,014	42,542	10,472	144,185	114,863	29,322
Gaston	15,498	11,709	3,789	42,223	31,614	10,609
Gates	82,095	76,223	5,872	222,244	205,802	16,442
Graham	8,713	0	8,713	24,396	0	24,396
Granville	23,665	3,920	19,745	65,870	10,584	55,286
Greene	45,549	29,504	16,045	124,587	79,661	44,926
Guilford	7,599	785	6,814	21,199	2,120	19,079
Halifax	106,053	87,403	18,650	288,208	235,988	52,220
Harnett	28,231	22,967	5,264	76,750	62,011	14,739
Haywood	23,735	4,130	19,605	66,045	11,151	54,894
Hertford	31,858	23,837	8,021	86,819	64,360	22,459
Hoke	40,502	38,208	2,294	109,585	103,162	6,423
Hyde	25,012	24,283	729	67,605	65,564	2,041
Iredell	5,939	2,142	3,797	16,415	5,783	10,632
Johnston	37,366	25,972	11,394	102,027	70,124	31,903
Jones	43,756	33,874	9,882	119,130	91,460	27,670
Lee	8,122	7,011	1,111	22,041	18,930	3,111
Lenoir	34,923	24,135	10,788	95,371	65,165	30,206
Lincoln	2,530	2,225	305	6,862	6,008	854

continued

Table A.13—Roundwood pulpwood production in North Carolina, 2010 (continued)

County[a]	All species	Softwood	Hardwood	All species	Softwood	Hardwood
		standard cords			*green tons*	
Macon	15,843	5,612	10,231	43,799	15,152	28,647
Martin	81,092	69,132	11,960	220,144	186,656	33,488
McDowell	33,467	13,408	20,059	92,367	36,202	56,165
Mecklenburg	2,576	1,711	865	7,042	4,620	2,422
Montgomery	40,710	38,772	1,938	110,110	104,684	5,426
Moore	44,164	38,368	5,796	119,823	103,594	16,229
Nash	41,348	33,465	7,883	112,428	90,356	22,072
New Hanover	4,095	3,296	799	11,136	8,899	2,237
Northampton	93,251	76,997	16,254	253,403	207,892	45,511
Onslow	130,550	99,207	31,343	355,619	267,859	87,760
Orange	4,787	20	4,767	13,402	54	13,348
Pamlico	57,875	38,301	19,574	158,220	103,413	54,807
Pasquotank	3,899	3,441	458	10,573	9,291	1,282
Pender	95,990	73,329	22,661	261,439	197,988	63,451
Perquimans	26,616	22,605	4,011	72,265	61,034	11,231
Person	12,170	147	12,023	34,061	397	33,664
Pitt	68,793	53,396	15,397	187,281	144,169	43,112
Polk	25,019	13,270	11,749	68,726	35,829	32,897
Randolph	12,588	585	12,003	35,188	1,580	33,608
Richmond	40,223	35,570	4,653	109,067	96,039	13,028
Robeson	81,096	58,187	22,909	221,250	157,105	64,145
Rockingham	56,792	14,321	42,471	157,586	38,667	118,919
Rowan	19,200	2,797	16,403	53,480	7,552	45,928
Rutherford	90,019	17,091	72,928	250,344	46,146	204,198
Sampson	95,088	66,329	28,759	259,613	179,088	80,525
Scotland	30,159	26,087	4,072	81,837	70,435	11,402
Stanly	9,133	6,893	2,240	24,883	18,611	6,272
Stokes	9,735	2,035	7,700	27,055	5,495	21,560
Surry	9,474	853	8,621	26,442	2,303	24,139
Tyrrell	14,269	12,180	2,089	38,735	32,886	5,849
Union	23,173	17,024	6,149	63,182	45,965	17,217
Vance	8,373	4,662	3,711	22,978	12,587	10,391
Wake	13,406	7,540	5,866	36,783	20,358	16,425
Warren	70,783	49,909	20,874	193,201	134,754	58,447
Washington	70,131	36,536	33,595	192,713	98,647	94,066
Watauga	659	63	596	1,839	170	1,669
Wayne	36,999	20,181	16,818	101,579	54,489	47,090
Wilkes	38,558	3,425	35,133	107,620	9,248	98,372
Wilson	96,419	85,614	10,805	261,412	231,158	30,254
Yadkin	5,956	1,225	4,731	16,555	3,308	13,247
Yancey	3,963	0	3,963	11,096	0	11,096
All counties	3,484,475	2,393,086	1,091,389	9,517,225	6,461,341	3,055,884

[a] Counties with no pulpwood production are omitted.

Table A.14—Roundwood pulpwood production in Oklahoma, 2010

County[a]	All species	Softwood	Hardwood	All species	Softwood	Hardwood
	standard cords			*green tons*		
Adair	18,031	695	17,336	50,418	1,877	48,541
Atoka	12,608	4,281	8,327	34,875	11,559	23,316
Bryan	4,448	31	4,417	12,452	84	12,368
Cherokee	13,358	812	12,546	37,321	2,192	35,129
Choctaw	38,028	19,316	18,712	104,547	52,153	52,394
Coal	511	0	511	1,431	0	1,431
Hughes	1,052	12	1,040	2,944	32	2,912
Johnston	3,064	11	3,053	8,578	30	8,548
Latimer	9,441	5,629	3,812	25,872	15,198	10,674
Le Flore	59,657	32,046	27,611	163,835	86,524	77,311
McCurtain	172,344	132,464	39,880	469,317	357,653	111,664
Pittsburg	6,676	592	6,084	18,633	1,598	17,035
Pushmataha	235,677	128,373	107,304	647,058	346,607	300,451
Sequoyah	1,469	121	1,348	4,101	327	3,774
All counties	576,364	324,383	251,981	1,581,382	875,834	705,548

[a] Counties with no pulpwood production are omitted.

Table A.15—Roundwood pulpwood production in South Carolina, 2010

County[a]	All species	Softwood	Hardwood	All species	Softwood	Hardwood
	standard cords			*green tons*		
Abbeville	40,343	18,844	21,499	111,076	50,879	60,197
Aiken	85,477	68,676	16,801	232,468	185,425	47,043
Allendale	58,936	41,042	17,894	160,916	110,813	50,103
Anderson	16,747	6,287	10,460	46,263	16,975	29,288
Bamberg	70,024	50,401	19,623	191,027	136,083	54,944
Barnwell	63,233	49,991	13,242	172,054	134,976	37,078
Beaufort	23,741	17,860	5,881	64,689	48,222	16,467
Berkeley	236,481	207,844	28,637	641,363	561,179	80,184
Calhoun	63,867	49,801	14,066	173,848	134,463	39,385
Charleston	82,419	71,112	11,307	223,662	192,002	31,660
Cherokee	18,994	16,200	2,794	51,563	43,740	7,823
Chester	126,634	95,217	31,417	345,054	257,086	87,968
Chesterfield	124,396	99,604	24,792	338,349	268,931	69,418
Clarendon	109,360	95,565	13,795	296,652	258,026	38,626
Colleton	213,338	152,208	61,130	582,126	410,962	171,164
Darlington	52,163	32,476	19,687	142,809	87,685	55,124
Dillon	99,306	46,169	53,137	273,440	124,656	148,784
Dorchester	149,406	118,304	31,102	406,507	319,421	87,086
Edgefield	93,625	76,860	16,765	254,464	207,522	46,942
Fairfield	281,685	260,106	21,579	762,707	702,286	60,421
Florence	97,418	26,136	71,282	270,157	70,567	199,590
Georgetown	140,125	133,891	6,234	378,961	361,506	17,455
Greenville	27,270	14,713	12,557	74,885	39,725	35,160
Greenwood	48,305	21,756	26,549	133,078	58,741	74,337
Hampton	126,777	96,314	30,463	345,344	260,048	85,296
Horry	71,289	47,615	23,674	194,848	128,561	66,287
Jasper	169,506	140,471	29,035	460,570	379,272	81,298
Kershaw	192,970	145,537	47,433	525,762	392,950	132,812
Lancaster	126,943	104,864	22,079	344,954	283,133	61,821
Laurens	51,782	27,788	23,994	142,211	75,028	67,183
Lee	99,896	77,814	22,082	271,928	210,098	61,830
Lexington	51,558	41,273	10,285	140,235	111,437	28,798
Marion	82,955	68,237	14,718	225,450	184,240	41,210
Marlboro	78,611	64,374	14,237	213,674	173,810	39,864
McCormick	25,756	18,909	6,847	70,226	51,054	19,172
Newberry	121,980	86,770	35,210	332,867	234,279	98,588
Oconee	36,985	25,493	11,492	101,009	68,831	32,178
Orangeburg	231,272	183,147	48,125	629,247	494,497	134,750
Pickens	33,048	18,619	14,429	90,672	50,271	40,401
Richland	116,661	84,962	31,699	318,154	229,397	88,757
Saluda	101,149	90,185	10,964	274,199	243,500	30,699
Spartanburg	46,641	20,118	26,523	128,583	54,319	74,264
Sumter	117,423	64,779	52,644	322,306	174,903	147,403
Union	194,843	151,634	43,209	530,397	09,412	120,985
Williamsburg	243,009	194,736	48,273	660,951	525,787	135,164
York	68,927	49,335	19,592	188,063	133,205	54,858
All counties	4,713,274	3,574,037	1,139,237	12,839,768	9,649,903	3,189,865

[a] Counties with no pulpwood production are omitted.

Table A.16—Roundwood pulpwood production in Tennessee, 2010

County[a]	All species	Softwood	Hardwood	All species	Softwood	Hardwood
	standard cords			*green tons*		
Anderson	12,343	474	11,869	34,513	1,280	33,233
Bedford	369	0	369	1,033	0	1,033
Benton	27,743	20,414	7,329	75,639	55,118	20,521
Bledsoe	22,000	8,885	13,115	60,712	23,990	36,722
Blount	4,568	898	3,670	12,701	2,425	10,276
Bradley	12,733	8,896	3,837	34,763	24,019	10,744
Campbell	32,354	422	31,932	90,549	1,139	89,410
Cannon	2,768	138	2,630	7,737	373	7,364
Carroll	36,145	6,800	29,345	100,526	18,360	82,166
Cheatham	499	0	499	1,397	0	1,397
Chester	29,158	19,983	9,175	79,644	53,954	25,690
Claiborne	15,712	0	15,712	43,994	0	43,994
Clay	2,509	605	1,904	6,965	1,634	5,331
Cocke	5,356	535	4,821	14,944	1,445	13,499
Coffee	9,307	1,230	8,077	25,937	3,321	22,616
Crockett	29	0	29	81	0	81
Cumberland	52,380	5,976	46,404	146,066	16,135	129,931
Davidson	61	0	61	171	0	171
Decatur	72,622	46,365	26,257	198,706	125,186	73,520
DeKalb	370	0	370	1,036	0	1,036
Dickson	26,071	1,005	25,066	72,899	2,714	70,185
Dyer	1,330	0	1,330	3,724	0	3,724
Fayette	10,060	7,393	2,667	27,429	19,961	7,468
Fentress	18,052	1,441	16,611	50,402	3,891	46,511
Franklin	14,415	226	14,189	40,339	610	39,729
Gibson	3,616	176	3,440	10,107	475	9,632
Giles	16,456	1,109	15,347	45,966	2,994	42,972
Grainger	501	134	367	1,390	362	1,028
Greene	596	30	566	1,666	81	1,585
Grundy	56,178	9,140	47,038	156,384	24,678	131,706
Hamilton	35,452	23,009	12,443	96,964	62,124	34,840
Hardeman	55,524	28,250	27,274	152,642	76,275	76,367
Hardin	44,477	24,214	20,263	122,114	65,378	56,736
Hawkins	13,699	11	13,688	38,356	30	38,326
Haywood	1,354	11	1,343	3,790	30	3,760
Henderson	35,255	11,681	23,574	97,546	31,539	66,007
Henry	26,762	14,725	12,037	73,462	39,758	33,704
Hickman	69,349	8,870	60,479	193,290	23,949	169,341
Houston	51,981	1,654	50,327	145,382	4,466	140,916
Humphreys	25,934	7,064	18,870	71,909	19,073	52,836
Jackson	759	255	504	2,100	689	1,411
Jefferson	762	0	762	2,134	0	2,134
Knox	5,808	2,682	3,126	15,994	7,241	8,753
Lauderdale	455	0	455	1,274	0	1,274
Lawrence	39,843	15,138	24,705	110,047	40,873	69,174
Lewis	81,075	11,624	69,451	225,848	31,385	194,463
Lincoln	3,270	0	3,270	9,156	0	9,156
Loudon	2,775	478	2,297	7,723	1,291	6,432
Macon	2,142	0	2,142	5,998	0	5,998
Madison	17,065	2,190	14,875	47,563	5,913	41,650
Marion	36,590	9,216	27,374	101,530	24,883	76,647
Marshall	11,346	404	10,942	31,729	1,091	30,638

continued

Table A.16—Roundwood pulpwood production in Tennessee, 2010 (continued)

County[a]	All species	Softwood	Hardwood	All species	Softwood	Hardwood
		standard cords			*green tons*	
Maury	7,360	224	7,136	20,586	605	19,981
McMinn	61,838	31,247	30,591	170,022	84,367	85,655
McNairy	54,073	22,030	32,043	149,201	59,481	89,720
Meigs	4,058	1,887	2,171	11,174	5,095	6,079
Monroe	27,492	12,136	15,356	75,764	32,767	42,997
Montgomery	465	0	465	1,302	0	1,302
Moore	2,547	0	2,547	7,132	0	7,132
Morgan	12,373	1,240	11,133	34,520	3,348	31,172
Obion	2,376	763	1,613	6,576	2,060	4,516
Overton	10,132	1,673	8,459	28,202	4,517	23,685
Perry	32,724	4,594	28,130	91,168	12,404	78,764
Polk	9,824	896	8,928	27,417	2,419	24,998
Putnam	7,061	1,818	5,243	19,589	4,909	14,680
Rhea	19,431	10,613	8,818	53,345	28,655	24,690
Roane	2,352	395	1,957	6,547	1,067	5,480
Rutherford	1,492	0	1,492	4,178	0	4,178
Scott	38,561	204	38,357	107,951	551	107,400
Sequatchie	26,819	17,434	9,385	73,350	47,072	26,278
Sevier	2,366	2,002	364	6,424	5,405	1,019
Shelby	6,337	2,323	4,014	17,511	6,272	11,239
Stewart	64,207	46,309	17,898	175,148	125,034	50,114
Sumner	193	0	193	540	0	540
Tipton	1,466	51	1,415	4,100	138	3,962
Unicoi	83	0	83	232	0	232
Union	3,967	646	3,321	11,043	1,744	9,299
Van Buren	44,096	10,257	33,839	122,443	27,694	94,749
Warren	21,363	6,160	15,203	59,200	16,632	42,568
Washington	31,934	0	31,934	89,415	0	89,415
Wayne	109,076	62,575	46,501	299,156	168,953	130,203
Weakley	14,066	6,322	7,744	38,752	17,069	21,683
White	19,966	6,645	13,321	55,241	17,942	37,299
Williamson	2,374	0	2,374	6,647	0	6,647
All counties	1,690,450	554,195	1,136,255	4,677,847	1,496,333	3,181,514

[a] Counties with no pulpwood production are omitted.

Table A.17—Roundwood pulpwood production in Texas, 2010

County[a]	All species	Softwood	Hardwood	All species	Softwood	Hardwood
	standard cords			*green tons*		
Anderson	4,395	3,632	763	11,942	9,806	2,136
Angelina	90,327	53,247	37,080	247,591	143,767	103,824
Bowie	61,403	32,253	29,150	168,703	87,083	81,620
Camp	9,574	3,891	5,683	26,418	10,506	15,912
Cass	274,259	109,043	165,216	757,021	294,416	462,605
Cherokee	77,912	53,281	24,631	212,826	143,859	68,967
Colorado	21	0	21	59	0	59
Fannin	5,845	0	5,845	16,366	0	16,366
Franklin	6,067	1,250	4,817	16,863	3,375	13,488
Gregg	5,061	859	4,202	14,085	2,319	11,766
Grimes	11	11	0	30	30	0
Hardin	151,392	119,951	31,441	411,903	323,868	88,035
Harris	167	110	57	457	297	160
Harrison	69,261	45,029	24,232	189,428	121,578	67,850
Henderson	478	456	22	1,293	1,231	62
Hopkins	3,518	29	3,489	9,847	78	9,769
Houston	16,627	4,306	12,321	46,125	11,626	34,499
Jasper	321,190	293,193	27,997	870,013	791,621	78,392
Jefferson	8	8	0	22	22	0
Lamar	5,473	1,484	3,989	15,176	4,007	11,169
Leon	3,637	0	3,637	10,184	0	10,184
Liberty	68,569	36,798	31,771	188,314	99,355	88,959
Marion	49,655	27,045	22,610	136,330	73,022	63,308
Montgomery	20,425	4,758	15,667	56,715	12,847	43,868
Morris	14,422	7,114	7,308	39,670	19,208	20,462
Nacogdoches	65,354	41,677	23,677	178,824	112,528	66,296
Newton	245,044	215,769	29,275	664,546	582,576	81,970
Orange	28,879	22,379	6,500	78,623	60,423	18,200
Panola	57,753	34,137	23,616	158,295	92,170	66,125
Polk	47,362	39,798	7,564	128,634	107,455	21,179
Red River	125,673	45,936	79,737	347,291	124,027	223,264
Rusk	12,816	7,769	5,047	35,108	20,976	14,132
Sabine	21,933	15,731	6,202	59,840	42,474	17,366
San Augustine	57,661	37,094	20,567	157,742	100,154	57,588
San Jacinto	27,238	4,344	22,894	75,832	11,729	64,103
Shelby	55,086	39,308	15,778	150,310	106,132	44,178
Smith	44,410	7,210	37,200	123,627	19,467	104,160
Titus	20,635	867	19,768	57,691	2,341	55,350
Trinity	19,383	19,373	10	52,335	52,307	28
Tyler	234,452	185,171	49,281	637,949	499,962	137,987
Upshur	37,995	15,726	22,269	104,813	42,460	62,353
Van Zandt	399	399	0	1,077	1,077	0
Walker	12,660	0	12,660	35,448	0	35,448
Wood	27,890	14,529	13,361	76,639	39,228	37,411
All counties	2,402,320	1,544,965	857,355	6,572,005	4,171,407	2,400,598

[a] Counties with no pulpwood production are omitted.

TableA.18—Roundwood pulpwood production in Virginia, 2010

County[a]	All species	Softwood	Hardwood	All species	Softwood	Hardwood
	standard cords			*green tons*		
Accomack	43	0	43	120	0	120
Albemarle	21,697	8,971	12,726	59,855	24,222	35,633
Alleghany	30,823	3,478	27,345	85,957	9,391	76,566
Amelia	66,212	44,171	22,041	180,977	119,262	61,715
Amherst	41,924	21,427	20,497	115,245	57,853	57,392
Appomattox	47,161	28,409	18,752	129,210	76,704	52,506
Augusta	8,747	2,495	6,252	24,243	6,737	17,506
Bath	13,534	1,285	12,249	37,767	3,470	34,297
Bedford	34,890	2,967	31,923	97,395	8,011	89,384
Bland	2,435	56	2,379	6,812	151	6,661
Botetourt	25,406	4,713	20,693	70,665	12,725	57,940
Brunswick	211,647	175,520	36,127	575,060	473,904	101,156
Buchanan	1,034	0	1,034	2,895	0	2,895
Buckingham	177,678	114,935	62,743	486,005	310,325	175,680
Campbell	22,899	1,787	21,112	63,939	4,825	59,114
Caroline	113,433	80,789	32,644	309,533	218,130	91,403
Carroll	3,304	1,020	2,284	9,149	2,754	6,395
Charles City	35,445	22,017	13,428	97,044	59,446	37,598
Charlotte	47,941	6,816	41,125	133,553	18,403	115,150
Chesapeake	6,541	1,269	5,272	18,188	3,426	14,762
Chesterfield	30,065	15,731	14,334	82,609	42,474	40,135
Clarke	516	467	49	1,398	1,261	137
Craig	6,009	455	5,554	16,780	1,229	15,551
Culpeper	14,302	12,461	1,841	38,800	33,645	5,155
Cumberland	55,340	32,992	22,348	151,652	89,078	62,574
Dickenson	62,617	79	62,538	175,319	213	175,106
Dinwiddie	57,527	23,562	33,965	158,719	63,617	95,102
Essex	37,318	26,575	10,743	101,833	71,753	30,080
Fairfax	2,911	823	2,088	8,068	2,222	5,846
Fauquier	13,295	8,695	4,600	36,357	23,477	12,880
Floyd	3,205	1,333	1,872	8,841	3,599	5,242
Fluvanna	21,865	14,586	7,279	59,763	39,382	20,381
Franklin	29,968	5,500	24,468	83,360	14,850	68,510
Frederick	11,578	4,691	6,887	31,950	12,666	19,284
Giles	312	0	312	874	0	874
Gloucester	18,672	12,732	5,940	51,008	34,376	16,632
Goochland	22,127	13,470	8,657	60,609	36,369	24,240
Grayson	1,347	64	1,283	3,765	173	3,592
Greene	4,592	2,416	2,176	12,616	6,523	6,093
Greensville	59,748	34,103	25,645	163,884	92,078	71,806
Halifax	32,746	208	32,538	91,668	562	91,106
Hampton	42	14	28	116	38	78
Hanover	49,818	39,042	10,776	135,586	105,413	30,173
Henrico	981	186	795	2,728	502	2,226
Henry	26,621	5,389	21,232	74,000	14,550	59,450
Highland	8,754	1,007	7,747	24,411	2,719	21,692
Isle of Wight	38,930	31,499	7,431	105,854	85,047	20,807
James City	5,249	1,256	3,993	14,571	3,391	11,180
King and Queen	44,926	33,331	11,595	122,460	89,994	32,466
King George	9,654	7,328	2,326	26,299	19,786	6,513
King William	27,712	19,226	8,486	75,671	51,910	23,761

continued

Table A.18—Roundwood pulpwood production in Virginia, 2010 (continued)

County[a]	All species	Softwood	Hardwood	All species	Softwood	Hardwood
	standard cords			green tons		
Lancaster	7,719	4,003	3,716	21,213	10,808	10,405
Lee	1,396	786	610	3,830	2,122	1,708
Loudoun	1,119	159	960	3,117	429	2,688
Louisa	97,838	60,361	37,477	267,911	162,975	104,936
Lunenburg	53,288	24,536	28,752	146,753	66,247	80,506
Madison	3,611	1,797	1,814	9,931	4,852	5,079
Mathews	12,538	6,864	5,674	34,420	18,533	15,887
Mecklenburg	70,558	46,191	24,367	192,944	124,716	68,228
Middlesex	9,882	3,996	5,886	27,270	10,789	16,481
Montgomery	9,930	818	9,112	27,723	2,209	25,514
Nelson	21,979	7,479	14,500	60,793	20,193	40,600
New Kent	8,405	4,193	4,212	23,115	11,321	11,794
Newport News	2,477	1,507	970	6,785	4,069	2,716
Northumberland	7,581	2,144	5,437	21,013	5,789	15,224
Nottoway	63,284	50,891	12,393	172,106	137,406	34,700
Orange	16,534	11,071	5,463	45,188	29,892	15,296
Page	2,615	1,295	1,320	7,193	3,497	3,696
Patrick	45,686	6,766	38,920	127,244	18,268	108,976
Pittsylvania	57,956	7,868	50,088	161,490	21,244	140,246
Powhatan	32,575	13,641	18,934	89,846	36,831	53,015
Prince Edward	27,063	3,011	24,052	75,476	8,130	67,346
Prince George	24,246	11,239	13,007	66,765	30,345	36,420
Prince William	1,908	1,562	346	5,186	4,217	969
Rappahannock	1,453	864	589	3,982	2,333	1,649
Richmond	33,801	19,154	14,647	92,728	51,716	41,012
Roanoke	2,944	751	2,193	8,168	2,028	6,140
Rockbridge	20,174	2,467	17,707	56,241	6,661	49,580
Rockingham	10,463	1,309	9,154	29,165	3,534	25,631
Russell	3,611	0	3,611	10,111	0	10,111
Scott	771	0	771	2,159	0	2,159
Shenandoah	5,116	1,857	3,259	14,139	5,014	9,125
Smyth	2,968	66	2,902	8,304	178	8,126
Southampton	140,907	103,597	37,310	384,180	279,712	104,468
Spotsylvania	22,380	15,666	6,714	61,097	42,298	18,799
Stafford	21,487	5,708	15,779	59,593	15,412	44,181
Suffolk	40,565	34,717	5,848	110,110	93,736	16,374
Surry	57,554	42,780	14,774	156,873	115,506	41,367
Sussex	64,939	50,849	14,090	176,744	137,292	39,452
Tazewell	9,592	14	9,578	26,856	38	26,818
Virginia Beach	4,659	2,562	2,097	12,789	6,917	5,872
Warren	1,443	606	837	3,980	1,636	2,344
Washington	414	0	414	1,159	0	1,159
Westmoreland	11,052	5,453	5,599	30,400	14,723	15,677
Wise	6,056	0	6,056	16,957	0	16,957
Wythe	911	29	882	2,548	78	2,470
York	751	410	341	2,062	1,107	955
All counties	2,655,740	1,432,383	1,223,357	7,292,838	3,867,437	3,425,401

[a] Counties with no pulpwood production are omitted.

Table A.19—Softwood roundwood pulpwood movement between States, 2010

Southeast

Imported from	Exported to										Roundwood production
	FL	GA	NC	SC	VA	AL	MD	PA	TN	Other[a]	
	standard cords										
Florida	2,814,257	405,857	0	0	0	54,945	0	0	0	0	3,275,059
Georgia	720,102	6,335,155	1,426	65,875	0	361,332	0	0	246,389	0	7,730,279
North Carolina	0	0	1,978,583	370,079	40,067	0	0	0	4,357	0	2,393,086
South Carolina	0	377,935	294,428	2,899,828	0	0	0	0	1,846	0	3,574,037
Virginia	0	0	341,009	715	908,278	0	105,003	75,712	0	1,666	1,432,383
Alabama	468,742	582,289	0	0	0	0	0	0	0	0	NA
Mississippi	37,916	0	0	0	0	0	0	0	0	0	NA
Tennessee	0	3,160	0	0	0	0	0	0	0	0	NA
West Virginia	0	0	0	0	3,016	0	0	0	0	0	NA
Other[b]	0	9	0	10	68	0	0	0	0	0	NA
Roundwood receipts	4,041,017	7,704,405	2,615,446	3,336,507	951,429						18,404,844

Total Southeast receipts = 18,648,804

South Central

Imported from	Exported to										Roundwood production
	AL	AR	KY	LA	MS	TN	TX/OK[c]	FL	GA	Other[a]	
	standard cords										
Alabama	4,122,715	0	0	1,985	225,583	131,773	0	468,742	582,289	0	5,533,087
Arkansas	0	1,443,267	0	226,385	11	0	350,042	0	0	0	2,019,705
Kentucky	0	0	26,668	0	0	9,167	0	0	0	4,303	40,138
Louisiana	0	77,360	0	3,511,829	10,638	0	296,353	0	0	0	3,896,180
Mississippi	279,186	6,236	0	698,906	3,282,815	464,258	0	37,916	0	0	4,769,317
Tennessee	66,132	0	51,351	0	0	433,552	0	0	3,160	0	554,195
Texas/Oklahoma[c]	0	130,867	0	245,254	0	0	1,493,227	0	0	0	1,869,348
Florida	54,945	0	0	0	0	0	0	0	0	0	NA
Georgia	361,332	0	0	0	0	246,389	0	0	0	0	NA
Illinois	0	0	1,986	0	0	0	0	0	0	0	NA
North Carolina	0	0	0	0	0	4,357	0	0	0	0	NA
South Carolina	0	0	0	0	0	1,846	0	0	0	0	NA
Other[b]	0	50	12,340	26	0	0	0	0	0	0	NA
Roundwood receipts	4,884,310	1,657,780	92,345	4,684,385	3,519,047	1,291,342	2,139,622				18,681,970

Total South Central receipts = 18,268,831

Note: Boxed numbers are retained roundwood volume processed by mills in the State in which it is harvested.

NA = not applicable.

[a] Other destinations include Ohio.

[b] Other sources include Maryland and Missouri.

[c] Values have been combined for confidentiality purposes.

Table A.20—Hardwood roundwood pulpwood movement between States, 2010

Southeast

Imported from	Exported to FL	GA	NC	SC	VA	AL	LA	MD	PA	TN	Other[a]	Roundwood production
						standard cords						
Florida	156,925	47,505	0	0	0	18,757	0	0	0	0	0	223,187
Georgia	6,179	1,239,314	6,152	12,996	0	162,003	1,472	0	0	125,959	7,457	1,561,532
North Carolina	0	66	742,392	118,267	150,508	0	0	0	0	79,162	994	1,091,389
South Carolina	0	118,143	66,965	954,129	0	0	0	0	0	0	0	1,139,237
Virginia	0	53,837	33,068	446	998,937	0	0	47,298	9,303	80,468	0	1,223,357
Alabama	8,132	61,315	0	0	0	0	0	0	0	0	0	NA
Maryland	0	0	0	0	984	0	0	0	0	0	0	NA
Mississippi	2,448	0	0	0	0	0	0	0	0	0	0	NA
Tennessee	0	0	97,810	1,248	0	0	0	0	0	0	0	NA
West Virginia	0	0	0	0	208,677	0	0	0	0	0	0	NA
Other[b]	0	73	9	2,992	1,232	0	0	0	0	0	0	NA
Roundwood receipts	173,684	1,520,253	946,396	1,090,078	1,360,338							5,238,702

Total Southeast receipts = 5,090,749

South Central

Imported from	AL	AR	KY	LA	MS	TN	TX/OK[c]	FL	GA	NC	SC	Other[d]	Roundwood production
						standard cords							
Alabama	2,290,597	0	52,289	0	0	15,905	10	8,132	61,315	0	0	0	2,428,248
Arkansas	0	1,042,303	0	84	0	0	208,518	0	0	0	0	0	1,250,905
Kentucky	759	1,867	259,716	226	0	63,818	0	0	0	0	1,243	16,630	344,259
Louisiana	0	188,047	0	462,200	5,641	0	183,164	0	0	0	0	0	839,052
Mississippi	499,811	284,799	141,698	338,060	226,069	51,664	8,161	2,448	0	0	0	0	1,552,710
Tennessee	367,667	147	168,176	0	0	501,207	0	0	0	97,810	1,248	0	1,136,255
Texas/Oklahoma[c]	0	354,773	0	36,797	0	0	717,733	0	15	9	9	0	1,109,336
Florida	18,757	0	0	0	0	0	0	0	0	0	0	0	NA
Georgia	162,003	6,458	0	1,472	0	125,959	999	0	0	0	0	0	NA
Illinois	0	0	14,961	0	0	0	0	0	0	0	0	0	NA
North Carolina	0	0	994	0	0	79,162	0	0	0	0	0	0	NA
Other[e]	1,398	930	100,618	55,884	0	80,817	12,187	0	0	0	0	0	NA
Roundwood receipts	3,340,992	1,879,324	738,452	894,723	231,710	918,532	1,130,772						8,660,765

Total South Central receipts = 9,134,505

Note: Boxed numbers are retained roundwood volume processed by mills in the State in which it is harvested.

NA = not applicable.

[a] Other destinations include Arkansas, Texas, and Kentucky.

[b] Other sources include Kentucky, Massachusetts, Missouri, Ohio, Oklahoma, and Wisconsin.

[c] Values have been combined for confidentiality purposes.

[d] Other destinations include Ohio.

[e] Other sources include Indiana, Missouri, New York, Ohio, Pennsylvania, Virginia, Wisconsin, and foreign.

Table A.21—Southern pulpmills, by process and capacity, 2010

Location	Map code[a]	Company	Pulping capacity, 24 hours				
			All processes	Sulfate	Groundwood and other mechanical	Semi-chemical	Soda and sulfite
					tons		
Alabama							
Clairborne[b]	[1,2]	Alabama River Companies	2,571	2,571	0	0	0
Jackson	[3]	Boise Cascade LLC	800	800	0	0	0
Courtland	[4]	International Paper Company	4,750	4,750	0	0	0
Demopolis	[5]	Rock-Tenn Company	1,135	1,135	0	0	0
Selma	[6]	International Paper Company	1,493	1,493	0	0	0
Naheola	[7]	Georgia-Pacific Corporation	1,850	1,850	0	0	0
Brewton	[8]	Georgia-Pacific Corporation	1,300	1,300	0	0	0
Coosa Pines	[9]	AbitibiBowater, Inc.	800	0	0	800	0
Pine Hill	[10]	International Paper Company	1,811	1,300	0	511	0
Cottonton	[11]	MeadWestvaco Corporation	2,300	2,300	0	0	0
Stevenson	[12]	Smurfit-Stone Container Corporation	750	0	0	750	0
Prattville	[13]	International Paper Company	3,162	3,162	0	0	0
		Total	22,722	20,661	0	2,061	0
Arkansas							
Pine Bluff	[14]	Delta Natural Kraft	450	450	0	0	0
Ashdown	[15]	Domtar Paper Co., LLC	2,450	2,450	0	0	0
Crossett	[16]	Georgia-Pacific Corporation	1,600	1,600	0	0	0
Morrilton	[17]	Green Bay Packaging, Inc.	800	800	0	0	0
Pine Bluff	[18]	Evergreen Packaging, Inc.	1,520	1,370	150	0	0
McGehee	[19]	Clearwater Paper Corp.	900	900	0	0	0
		Total	7,720	7,570	150	0	0
Florida							
Perry	[20]	Buckeye Florida, LP	1,200	1,200	0	0	0
Cantonment	[21]	International Paper Company	1,903	1,903	0	0	0
Palatka	[22]	Georgia-Pacific Corporation	1,250	1,250	0	0	0
Fernandina Beach	[23]	Rayonier, Inc.	475	0	0	0	475
Fernandina Beach	[24]	Smurfit-Stone Container Corporation	2,200	2,200	0	0	0
Panama City	[25]	Smurfit-Stone Container Corporation	1,635	1,635	0	0	0
		Total	8,663	8,188	0	0	475
Georgia							
Augusta	[26]	Augusta Newsprint Company	1,100	0	1,100	0	0
Augusta	[27]	International Paper Company	2,025	2,025	0	0	0
Brunswick	[28]	Georgia-Pacific Corporation	2,450	2,450	0	0	0
Cedar Springs	[29]	Georgia-Pacific Corporation	2,825	2,300	0	525	0
Rome	[30]	Temple-Inland, Inc.	2,250	2,250	0	0	0
Riceboro	[31]	Interstate Paper LLC	780	780	0	0	0
Jesup	[32]	Rayonier, Inc.	1,750	1,750	0	0	0
Valdosta	[33]	Packaging Corporation of America	1,419	1,419	0	0	0
Macon	[34]	Graphic Packaging International, Inc.	1,450	1,450	0	0	0
Savannah	[35]	International Paper Company	2,600	2,600	0	0	0
Oglethorpe	[36]	Weyerhaeuser Company	1,155	1,155	0	0	0
Port Wentworth	[37]	Weyerhaeuser Company	975	975	0	0	0
		Total	20,779	19,154	1,100	525	0

continued

Table A.21—Southern pulpmills, by process and capacity, 2010 (continued)

Location	Map code[a]	Company	Pulping capacity, 24 hours				
			All processes	Sulfate	Groundwood and other mechanical	Semi-chemical	Soda and sulfite
			tons				
Kentucky							
Wickliffe	[38]	NewPage Corporation	850	850	0	0	0
Hawesville	[39]	Domtar Paper Co., LLC	1,400	1,400	0	0	0
		Total	2,250	2,250	0	0	0
Louisiana							
DeRidder	[40]	Boise Packaging and Newsprint	1,975	1,300	675	0	0
Bogalusa	[41]	Temple-Inland, Inc.	2,205	2,205	0	0	0
Port Hudson	[42]	Georgia-Pacific Corporation	1,920	1,920	0	0	0
Mansfield	[43]	International Paper Company	2,958	1,957	0	1,001	0
West Monroe	[44]	Graphic Packaging International, Inc.	1,628	1,628	0	0	0
Hodge	[45]	Smurfit-Stone Container Corporation	1,500	1,500	0	0	0
Campti	[46]	International Paper Company	1,134	1,134	0	0	0
		Total	13,320	11,644	675	1,001	0
Mississippi							
Monticello	[47]	Georgia-Pacific Corporation	2,500	2,500	0	0	0
New Augusta	[48]	Koch Industries	1,550	1,550	0	0	0
Vicksburg	[49]	International Paper Company	1,404	1,404	0	0	0
Grenada	[50]	AbitibiBowater, Inc.	800	0	800	0	0
Columbus	[51a]	Weyerhaeuser Company	1,450	1,450	0	0	0
Columbus	[51b]	Domtar, Inc.	350	0	350	0	0
		Total	8,054	6,904	1,150	0	0
North Carolina							
Roaring River	[52]	Louisiana-Pacific Corporation	475	0	475	0	0
Canton	[53]	Evergreen Packaging, Inc.	1,600	1,600	0	0	0
Roanoke Rapids	[54]	KapStone Kraft Paper Corp.	1,500	1,500	0	0	0
Riegelwood	[55]	International Paper Company	2,545	2,545	0	0	0
New Bern	[56]	Weyerhaeuser Company	900	900	0	0	0
Plymouth	[57]	Domtar, Inc.	1,250	1,250	0	0	0
		Total	8,270	7,795	475	0	0
Oklahoma							
Valliant	[58]	International Paper Company	2,075	1,582	0	493	0
		Total	2,075	1,582	0	493	0
South Carolina							
Catawba	[59]	AbitibiBowater, Inc.	2,100	1,500	600	0	0
Georgetown	[60]	International Paper Company	1,246	1,246	0	0	0
Hartsville	[61]	Sonoco Products Company	300	0	0	300	0
Florence	[62]	Smurfit-Stone Container Corporation	1,530	1,530	0	0	0
Eastover	[63]	International Paper Company	1,927	1,927	0	0	0
Charleston	[64]	KapStone Charleston Kraft LLC	2,080	2,080	0	0	0
Bennettsville	[65]	Domtar Paper Company, Inc.	1,000	1,000	0	0	0
		Total	10,183	9,283	600	300	0

continued

Table A.21—Southern pulpmills, by process and capacity, 2010 (continued)

Location	Map code[a]	Company	Pulping capacity, 24 hours				
			All processes	Sulfate	Groundwood and other mechanical	Semi-chemical	Soda and sulfite
			tons				
Tennessee							
Calhoun	[66]	AbitibiBowater, Inc.	1,450	1,000	450	0	0
New Johnsonville	[67]	Temple-Inland, Inc.	580	0	0	580	0
Kingsport	[68]	Domtar Paper Co., LLC	850	0	0	0	850
Counce	[69]	Packaging Corporation of America	1,950	1,950	0	0	0
Knoxville	[70]	Tamko Building Products, Inc.	125	0	125	0	0
		Total	4,955	2,950	575	580	850
Texas							
Texarkana	[71]	International Paper Company	1,900	1,900	0	0	0
Orange	[72]	Inland Paperboard and Packaging	1,887	1,887	0	0	0
Diboll	[73]	Temple-Inland, Inc.	500	0	500	0	0
Silsbee	[74]	MeadWestvaco Texas LP	1,650	1,650	0	0	0
		Total	5,937	5,437	500	0	0
Virginia							
Ashland	[75]	White Birch Paper Co.	880	0	880	0	0
West Point	[76]	Smurfit-Stone Container Corporation	1,700	1,700	0	0	0
Jarratt	[77]	Georgia-Pacific Corporation	400	0	400	0	0
Big Island	[78]	Georgia-Pacific Corporation	864	0	0	864	0
Hopewell	[79]	Smurfit-Stone Container Corporation	1,030	1,030	0	0	0
Franklin	[80]	International Paper Company	574	574	0	0	0
Riverville	[81]	Greif Packaging, LLC	600	0	0	600	0
Covington	[82]	MeadWestvaco Corporation	2,100	2,100	0	0	0
		Total	8,148	5,404	1,280	1,464	0
Total South			123,076	108,822	6,505	6,424	1,325

[a] Corresponds to numbers at locations on the mill capacity map (fig. 7).

[b] This is pulping capacity for two mills at this site.

Table A.22—Other mills using southern pulpwood in 2010, by process and capacity

Location	Company	Pulping capacity, 24 hours				
		All processes	Sulfate	Groundwood and other mechanical	Semi-chemical	Soda and sulfite
		tons				
Maryland						
Luke	NewPage Corporation	850	850			
Ohio						
Chillicothe	Glatfelter Company	1,785	1,785			
Pennsylvania						
Spring Grove	Glatfelter Company	700	700